Retirement Issues, Plans and Lifestyles Series

CHALLENGES WOMEN FACE IN RETIREMENT SECURITY

RETIREMENT ISSUES, PLANS AND LIFESTYLES SERIES

Social Security Solvency
Jeffrey K. Bain (Editor)
2009. ISBN 978-1-60692-833-2

Challenges Women Face In Retirement Security
Jean B. Larou (Editor)
2009. ISBN 978-1-60741-747-7

Retirement Issues, Plans and Lifestyles Series

CHALLENGES WOMEN FACE IN RETIREMENT SECURITY

JEAN B. LAROU
EDITOR

Nova Science Publishers, Inc.
New York

For permission to use material from this book please contact us:
Telephone 631-231-7269; Fax 631-231-8175
Web Site: http://www.novapublishers.com

NOTICE TO THE READER

The Publisher has taken reasonable care in the preparation of this book, but makes no expressed or implied warranty of any kind and assumes no responsibility for any errors or omissions. No liability is assumed for incidental or consequential damages in connection with or arising out of information contained in this book. The Publisher shall not be liable for any special, consequential, or exemplary damages resulting, in whole or in part, from the readers' use of, or reliance upon, this material.

Independent verification should be sought for any data, advice or recommendations contained in this book. In addition, no responsibility is assumed by the publisher for any injury and/or damage to persons or property arising from any methods, products, instructions, ideas or otherwise contained in this publication.

This publication is designed to provide accurate and authoritative information with regard to the subject matter covered herein. It is sold with the clear understanding that the Publisher is not engaged in rendering legal or any other professional services. If legal or any other expert assistance is required, the services of a competent person should be sought. FROM A DECLARATION OF PARTICIPANTS JOINTLY ADOPTED BY A COMMITTEE OF THE AMERICAN BAR ASSOCIATION AND A COMMITTEE OF PUBLISHERS.

LIBRARY OF CONGRESS CATALOGING-IN-PUBLICATION DATA
Available upon request

ISBN: 978-1-60741-747-7

Published by Nova Science Publishers, Inc. ✢ New York

CONTENTS

PREFACE

This book focuses on women and retirement. Women aged 65 and over will account for a growing segment of the U.S. population over the next several decades. Despite increases in women's workforce behavior in the past 65 years, elderly women have persistently high rates of poverty. Thus, it is important to understand the differences between men's and women's retirement income, and how women may fare given future reforms to Social Security and pensions. Preparing for retirement and achieving financial security are daunting tasks for all Americans to be sure; however, women face many unique challenges. Women still perform the primary caretaker role in our society. As a result, many women spend significant periods of time out of the workforce raising children or taking care of elderly parents, significantly diluting their earning power. Women are also more likely to work part-time or work in industries where employers are less likely to offer retirement benefits. And women generally earn less than men. In 2004, women earned 77 cents for every dollar earned by men. All of these factors have a significant impact on what women receive from Social Security and pension, as well as what they are able to accumulate through personal savings. This income gap is further exacerbated by the fact that women generally live longer than men, and therefore, need to stretch their income over a longer period of time.

This book consists of public domain documents which have been located, gathered, combined, reformatted, and enhanced with a subject index, selectively edited and bound to provide easy access.

In: Challenges Women Face in Retirement Security
Editor: Jean B. Larou, pp. 1-3
ISBN: 978-1-60741-747-7

Chapter 1

TESTIMONY OF JEAN CHATZKY, BEFORE THE SPECIAL COMMITTEE ON AGING, UNITED STATES SENATE, MARCH 15, 2006*

Chairman Smith, Ranking Member Kohl, thank you so much for inviting me to address your committee here today. It is an honor and privilege, in particular because the problem you are discussing this morning—the financial security of America's women—carries such importance to me both professionally and personally. And it is quite a problem:

According to the 2005 Retirement Confidence Survey conducted for the Employee Benefit Research Institute:

- Only 40 percent of women have even tried to calculate the amount of money they will need to live in retirement.
- Of those that have, most seem to be vastly underestimating their true retirement needs. Nearly 40 percent believe they will need less than $250,000 to live through retirement—a figure that works out to roughly $10,000 annually for the 20 to 25 year period they expect to live in retirement.
- Equally discouraging, just 59 percent of women are actively saving for retirement, which means that 41 percent are not, with only 36 percent contributing to a workplace retirement savings plan.
- All in all, it is not surprising that just 35 percent of women believe they will have enough money to pay for their most basic expenses in retirement, and an even slimmer share—just 23 percent—believe they will have enough to live comfortably during what are supposed to be their golden years. When you ask what percent of women believe they'll have enough money to fund their healthcare and long-term care expenses, the percentages are even more discouraging.

I was asked here this morning not simply to outline this crisis—and I do believe it is a crisis—but to offer specific solutions that could help women, in particular, meet their retirement needs. What many people do not understand about women is we possess innate

* This is an edited, reformatted and augmented version of testimony before the United States Senate Special Committee on Aging, March 15, 2006

qualities that make us spectacular investors of our own money—once we step up to the plate. Researchers from the University of California Davis looked into the discount brokerage records of thousands of investors, comparing those of women to those of men and found:

- Women are far less likely than men to hold a losing investment too long.
- Women don't wait too long to sell winning investments. Men do.
- Men are much more likely to put all—or at least too many—of their investment eggs in one basket. Women are more likely to diversify.
- Men trade securities so often it's a drag on their investment returns, women buy and hold to their advantage.
- And when women do make investing mistakes—we learn from them. We are much less likely than men to repeat destructive behavior more than once.

The upshot of all of that positive behavior? Women make more money on their investments than men. Unfortunately not enough of us are in it. And once we are, because we leave the workforce so often to care for children or older parents, our stop-and-start retirement funds don't grow to be as large as they could. A few simple changes to the way most retirement funds are implemented could change that.

First, change the defaults. Today, more than 20 years after the introduction of the 401(k), 30 percent of employees still choose not to sign up. In doing so they leave $30 billion annually in employer matching dollars on the table. Why are they making this mistake? Often because they do not understand the golden opportunity before them. That is why I believe investing in 401 (k)s and other defined contribution plans should be opt-out rather than opt-in. In other words employers should be able to assume this is something that employees are going to do. This will, research shows, boost participation to 90 percent and force those who do not want to participate to actively consider their choice.

Second, defined contribution plan contributions should increase automatically as an employee's wages rise over the years. This is a fairly new mechanism that some companies are putting in place. Contributions start at 3 percent and rise at a rate of 1 percentage point a year. Today only 25 percent of large companies have automatic escalation. It should be mandatory.

Third, an age-appropriate portfolio should also be automatic. One of the problems women investors, in particular face, is our reluctance to take risks. Unfortunately, a lifetime of savings in low risk/low reward money market and bond funds will not fund a secure retirement for most American women. The default should instead be a target-date retirement or lifecycle fund that automatically adjusts the underlying investment mix based on a woman's self-selected retirement date.

Fourth, education should be part of the IRA rollover process. I applaud the recent change that made IRA rollovers the default for plan balances over $1,000. However, while rolling over is good—rolling over and continuing to contribute is far better. Anyone rolling into an IRA should be educated on the opportunity they have to continue to make retirement contributions into a traditional, Roth or Spousal IRA on an automatic basis. Making the continuation of contributions part of the exit interview process means that a woman leaving the workforce has one less cumbersome step to take. Anything that simplifies the process insures greater participation.

These four changes will go a long way to insuring the retirement of the women who work for mid-size to large companies and other organizations that offer retirement plans. However, this still leaves self-employed women and women who are not in the traditional workforce (with two kids at home, I completely understand that stay-at-home moms work as hard if not harder than I do) in a lurch.

Here is what we know: Self-employment is of great appeal to women who want to be able to take care of their children, take care of their parents and still earn a living. That flexibility is one key reason why women start businesses at twice the rate of men. Self-employed individuals are less likely to save for retirement. Now, I am not schooled in the ways the government operates—so please forgive me if these next suggestions are naïve or reaching. But I believe there must be some way for the government—just like a large company—to be able to offer these women a default option that insures they are putting some of their own money away for retirement. Yes, there are incentives. But the incentives aren't doing it. I would suggest that the IRS and the Social Security Administration both be asked to consider whether either could be the funnel that drives additional dollars into a place where they can be saved—and grown.

Thank you.

In: Challenges Women Face in Retirement Security
Editor: Jean B. Larou, pp. 5-11

ISBN: 978-1-60741-747-7

Chapter 2

TESTIMONY OF SARA COLE HART, BEFORE THE UNITED STATES SENATE SPECIAL COMMITTEE ON AGING, MARCH 15, 2006*

Good morning Chairman Smith, from the great state of Oregon, Ranking Member Kohl and Members of the Committee. I appreciate the opportunity to discuss the important issue of the special challenges facing women in retirement.

Today, one out of four older women lives in or near the poverty level, according to the Older Women's League (OWL). Too many women rely on Social Security as their sole source of income. While the pension crisis is real, aging does not have to signify a decline in financial, physical or mental capacity. However the fact is that women in America, particularly women from economically or educationally disadvantaged backgrounds and women from racial or ethnic minorities are confronted with a serious, and often certain, challenge of living in poverty as they age. In fact, data show that one-fifth of elderly unmarried women and one-third of elderly women of color were in poverty in 1998.

Many studies and data analyses from some of the most credible organizations have examined this issue and all agree on the basic reasons why this is true. While I will review the various elements that conspire to create this crisis, I do not intend to spend this valuable time to discuss what has already been so thoroughly documented. Instead, I would rather speak to the potential solutions and answers that are within our grasp if we are serious about addressing this crisis.

The power of government taking action to establish a national retirement policy, partnered with private employers, can change millions of lives.

---

* This is an edited, reformatted and augmented version of testimony before the United States Senate Special Committee on Aging, March 15, 2006.

REVIEW OF THE REASONS WOMEN ARE MORE LIKELY TO END THEIR LIFE IN A STATE OF POVERTY

- The two main elements in determining an ultimate retirement income from a private pension plan or from Social Security are compensation levels throughout a worker's years of labor and the number of years in the full-time workforce.
    - Women tend to have higher incidence of interrupted (non-contiguous) employment as a result of their frequent role as primary caregivers of children and, later, elderly family members [1]. Entering and leaving the workforce and working for multiple employers, often result in women not achieving vesting in a retirement benefit.
    - Women earn less than do men [2]. This is attributable to multiple factors including education and career interruptions, higher prevalence of part- time work [3], and frequency of working for smaller employers in lower paid positions, not covered by a private pension plan.
- The socio-economic continuum has changed. Traditionally a woman relied on her husband for financial support and the single or elderly were embraced and cared for within the fabric of extended family. With rising divorce rates, prevalence of households headed by single women and increasingly mobile lifestyles of people of all ages, this no longer holds true [4]. The fact is that there is not enough money leftover after paying bills to save for retirement for most Americans.
- The tenuous financial status of elderly women is also related to marital status, race and ethnicity [5].
- Women are less prepared for retirement and are more intimidated about financial issues than men [6].
- The life expectancy of a female is longer than for a male [7]. This single demographic fact presents four distinct issues.
    - A woman must accumulate a larger nest egg during her working years to last through her longer lifetime.
    - A woman is disproportionately affected by loss of purchasing power due to inflation.
    - Longer life often results in significantly more serious or debilitating health problems, leading to higher medical expense and the probability of losing independence, requiring long term care or assisted living [8].
    - A widowed elderly woman is subject to the loss of her spouse's pension income and reduced Social Security benefits [9].

RECOMMENDATIONS FOR SOLUTIONS TO THE PENSION CRISIS FACED BY WOMEN

Support and encourage education, including a financial curriculum, beginning in primary school. In order to continue to grow the economy and achieve optimal productivity, employers must have an available resource of educated, trained individuals. Addressing the retirement issues facing women must begin as early as possible in order to mitigate the lost opportunities faced by lack of a strong education.

Make the EGTRRA pension and retirement savings provisions permanent, permitting Americans to save more in employer plans and IRAs. EGTRRA provides significant administrative relief to employers who sponsor plans and enhances the portability among various plans. Women are particularly benefited by the Saver's Credit, which assists low-income savers and by catch-up contributions that permit older workers to save more.

Federal income tax code discourages saving. Savings opportunities must be simplified and incentives for saving must be established. Employers are constrained by cumbersome pension and benefit regulations imposed by IRC, ERISA (and the erosion of ERISA protection) and ADEA. Employers need flexibility in age and service eligibility to maintain a retirement benefit.

Women covered by employer plans will benefit from the shift to a 401(k) or defined contribution plan arrangements because their structure supports savings accumulation during earlier years of employment. Congress should promote the establishment of a 401(k) type benefit at a federal level, allowing individuals or small business to take advantage of simplified administration and lower costs. Additionally there are several proposals in play right now that have the potential to severely undermine the chance of achieving a successful retirement.

- Help employers and individuals obtain some type of annuity which assists in the protection of income during one's lifetime. Lump sum payments often jeopardize retirement income security, especially for women who live longer.
- Do not support proposals that make it easier for active employees to take money out of their retirement savings programs for any reason. Workers have historically understood that defined benefit plan accumulations were not available for pre-retirement purposes. Defined contribution assets should be treated the same way. Do not adopt House sponsored distribution for qualified reservists, as this short term proposition will have long-term negative effects.
- Strengthen rules promoting a roll-over from an employer sponsored benefit to an eligible IRA or other qualified retirement vehicle. Increase disincentives for taking distributions prior to retirement.
- Early in the initiation of 401(k) plans, it was deemed necessary to offer loans and hardship withdrawals in order to ensure participation. With the prevalence of defined contribution plans, loans and withdrawals undermine future retirement income security. Curtailment of these types of withdrawals is crucial and education about the adverse effects of early withdrawals is essential.
- Support auto enrollment and auto increases into an employer's 401(k) plan and eliminate the ERISA preemption of state law restricting auto enrollment. Establish a safe harbor.
- Expand 404 (c) relief. Urge the DOL to affirm permissible asset classes and investment types.
- Add a fiduciary safe harbor for employers who select qualified independent investment advisors to assist workers. Studies indicate that women tend to invest more conservatively than men, receiving lower rates of return from their investment

over time, thus reducing the amount of savings they have at retirement. The addition of investment advice is invaluable.

- Promote changes to ERISA, the tax code and labor code that simplify and permit more flexibility. There are so many required notices that even participants don't pay attention.
- Support expanded benefit statements and the DOL website retirement planning tools.
- Simplify 5500 reporting for small plans.

The employer sponsored defined benefit system is in serious financial trouble, jeopardizing the pensions of millions of workers. The PBGC has a substantial deficit. However, the concept of "insurance" in the PBGC is broken with the few DB sponsors remaining required to pay higher premiums and submit to substantial administrative, accounting, reporting and funding changes. The increased volatility produced by the combination of reduced smoothing, the elimination or restriction of credit balances cause further disincentive for employers to continue to sponsor a DB plan. Employers also question the fairness of reform allowances for the particular industries.

Resolve the Social Security funding issue. Benefits as a share of workers' earnings are expected to decline in the future. In addition, Medicare premiums - which are subtracted from Social Security checks - are expected to rise rapidly. Social Security benefits may be further reduced to solve a long-term funding shortfall. Eliminate rules and incentives that discourage employees from continuing to work beyond traditional Social Security retirement age. The current Social Security system contains many benefits that must be maintained and strengthened, including full cost of living adjustments, guaranteed lifetime benefits, a progressive benefit formula, spousal and widow benefits, and disability and survivor benefits. Social Security improvements must maintain these guaranteed benefits and consider the inequity of pension benefits and retirement security for women.

Support Social Security credits for time spent as non-paid caregivers, funded by means testing for wealthier retirees. Consider a type of retirement account open to people without earned income, so that caregivers could hold something in their name other than an IRA.

Encourage implementation of Phased Retirement programs that match the reality of today's aging workforce. Pension regulations currently prohibit defined benefit plans from offering benefits before normal retirement date. Employers are facing labor and talent shortages. Recognize that the traditional concept of retirement is changing from work-save-retire model and being replaced by a lifestyle change. Gradual transition keeps talent in workforce and helps employers retain productive workers while transitioning into retirement by reduced hours and responsibility. Seasoned employees want to continue to make a difference. Support regulations to eliminate confusion and allow for establishment of phased retirement.

Employers are looking to Congress to affirm established precedent in Hybrid plans as well as settle the issues surrounding these plans on a prospective basis. The continued uncertainty is a strong deterrent to committing to sponsoring a Hybrid type plan.

Women face special challenges in finding a new job, career, employment path and maintaining a place in the workforce to become economically self-sufficient. Congress must support maximization of ongoing training opportunities that balance the requirements of a modern workforce with the income, civic, family and social needs. Tax incentives for employers to hire and train women returning to the workforce are undoubtedly a win-win cause and are a solution to the underutilization of women's talent.

Today with so much attention focused on the issue of retirement and pension reform, we have a meaningful opportunity to strengthen not strangle employer sponsored retirement systems, thereby offering stability to women and other workers. If Congress fails to enact a national retirement policy that recognizes the special needs of women it is tantamount to sanctioning poverty in old age as a natural result.

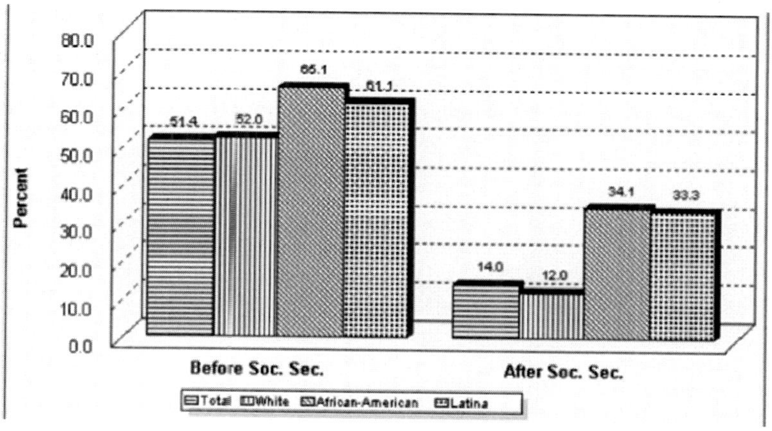

Source: These data are result of analyses by the Center on Budget and Policy Priorities using Current Population Survey data collected by the Bureau of the Census. The measures of poverty in this chart differ from the official poverty mearure. The poverty rates "before Social Security" were determined by counting only income from social means-tested benefits. The poverty rates "after Social Security" were determined by counting income from social insurance and Social Security; benefits from means-tested programs were not counted. By contrast, the official poverty measure all cash income. Including all government cash benefits. Benefits not in the form of cash (e.g. food stams) are not counted.

Figure 1. Proportion of Elderly Women Who Were Poor, by Race and Ethnicity, 1994-1998.

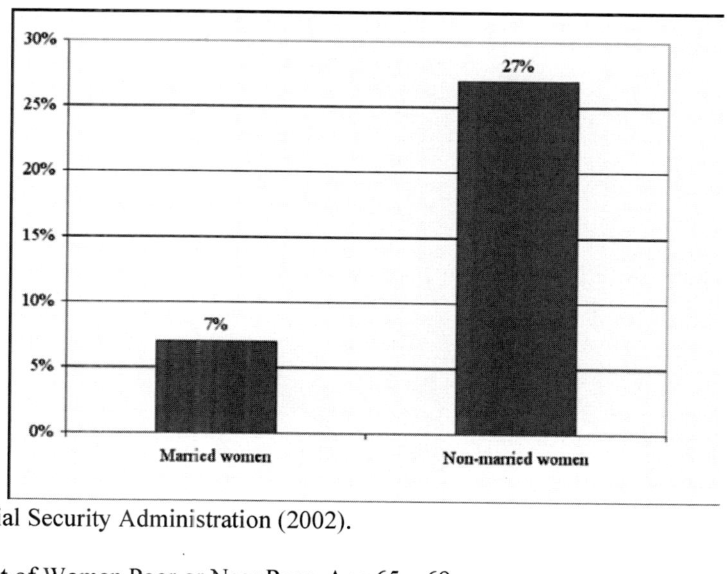

Source: US Social Security Administration (2002).

Figure 2. Percent of Women Poor or Near Poor, Age 65 – 69.

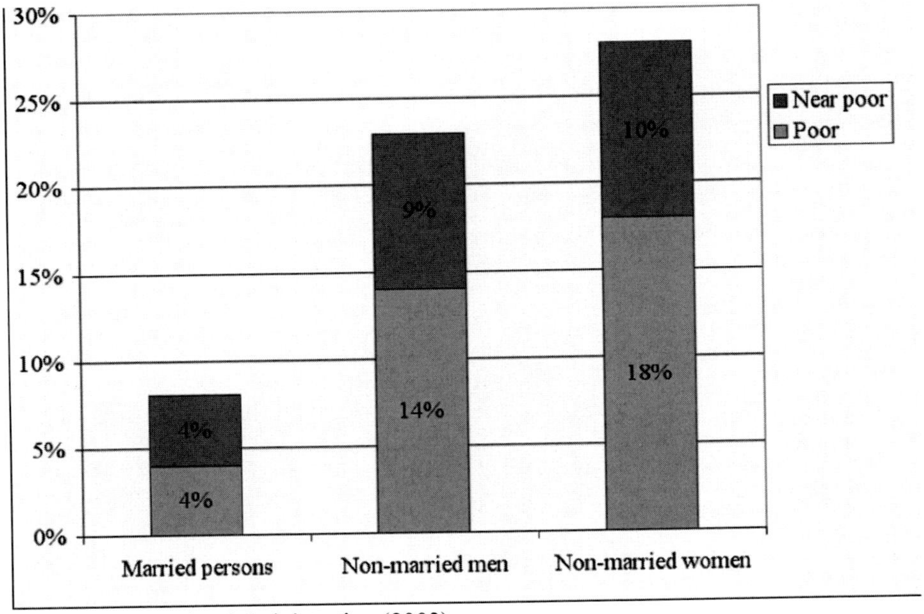

Source: US Social Security Administration (2003).

Figure 3. Life Expectancy at Age 65.

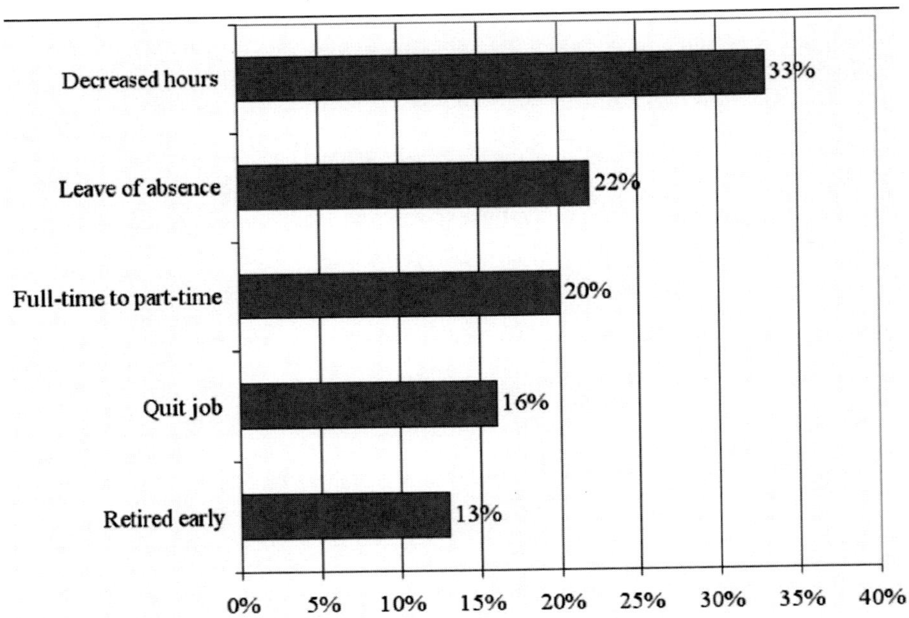

Source: Metropolitan Life Insurance Company (1999).

Figure 4. Effects of Caregiving on Work Schedule.

REFERENCES

[1] Women on average spend 10 years away from the workforce, for these and other reasons, versus one year for men. Financially, this results in lower overall earnings and smaller pension and Social Security benefits. For every year a woman stays out of the workforce, it will take her five years to recover lost income, pension coverage, and career advancement.

[2] Bureau of Labor and Census Bureau statistics from 1999 reveal that females age 25–34 earned a median income of $18,396, contrasted to males' median income of $29,864. Women 25 years and older with at least a bachelor's degree earned a median income of $31,642, while men in that same category earned a median income of $52,240. The weekly earnings gap equaled 23.5% and the annual earnings gap was 27.8% between females and males. Annual earnings for women working full time amounted to 72.2% of men's annual earnings.

[3] About twenty-five percent of all women work part time, compared to about ten percent of men, and are most likely to work part time when they have children at home. Women spend fewer years in the workforce, an average of 32 years, contrasted to an average of 44 years for men.

[4] Divorce and the problem of default on child support payments is a national crisis disproportionately affecting women and their ability to participate fully in the workplace and accumulate retirement savings. A U.S. Census Bureau report, Child Support for Custodial Mothers and Fathers, determined that out of 14 million custodial parents approximately 85% were women and 15% were men. Fewer than half received their full court-ordered child support payments. Custodial parents were due about $30 billion, with mothers due $26.4 billion and fathers $2.7 billion. The burden of child and household support falls more often to women with single incomes. Studies show that the average annual income for a divorced midlife woman is only $11,000.

[5] According to the Center on Budget and Policy priorities data using 1999 data collected by Bureau of Census.

[6] A 1997 study by Dreyfus and the National Center for Women and Retirement Research found that 33% of women investors avoided making decisions out of fear of making a mistake, versus 22% of the male investors. Women often defer financial decisions and money management to the men in their lives.

[7] On average, a woman retiring at age 55 can expect to live another 27 years, 4 years longer than a man retiring at the same age. With advances in healthcare during this century, life expectancies have continued to rise. More people reach the traditional retirement age of 65 than in the past and life expectancy during retirement has increased. In 1900, the average life expectancy for women was 47 years of age. Only one person in 25 survived to age 60 and women lived shorter lives due to childbirth, according to the U.S. Bureau of the Census. However, by 1950, life expectancy for women averaged at 71 and 65 for men. In 1990, females reaching the age of 65 were expected to live just over 19 years longer and men, on the average, lived 15 more years after the age of 65.

[8] Women are twice as likely as men to live in a nursing home and will spend more years and a larger percentage of their lifetime disabled.

[9] Women tend to marry older men; consequently, seven out of ten women, whose marriages remain intact, will outlive their husbands. Many of those women will be widows for fifteen to twenty years. The Administration on Aging notes that over half the elderly widows now living in poverty were not living in poverty before their husbands died.

In: Challenges Women Face in Retirement Security
Editor: Jean B. Larou, pp. 13-21
ISBN: 978-1-60741-747-7

Chapter 3

TESTIMONY OF M. CINDY HOUNSELL, WOMEN'S INSTITUTE FOR A SECURE RETIREMENT, BEFORE THE SENATE SPECIAL COMMITTEE ON AGING, HEARING ON WOMEN'S RETIREMENT INCOME, MARCH 15, 2006*

INTRODUCTION

Chairman Smith, Senator Kohl, distinguished members of the Committee, thank you for inviting me to discuss the issue of closing the retirement income gap for women in the United States.

My name is Cindy Hounsell. I am president of the Women's Institute for a Secure Retirement (WISER), a nonprofit organization dedicated to ensuring the security of women's retirement income through outreach, partnerships, and policy advocacy.

WISER commends the Committee for examining the unique challenges faced by women in preparing for and managing their retirement years. My testimony will briefly cover the reasons women face dramatic economic insecurity in retirement, and will offer recommendations for actions that individuals, employers and policymakers can take to make sure that women have access to employer-sponsored plans, access to spousal benefits and that the holes are plugged to mitigate the risks of losing retirement income along the life-course.

A COMING CRISIS

As you are well aware, much attention has been paid to the retirement income insecurity of American workers generally. The issues faced by women in particular are compounded by a number of factors, the result of which paints a startling post-retirement picture for millions of women who have worked their entire lives in one capacity or another.

* This is an edited, reformatted and augmented version of testimony before the United States Senate Special Committee on Aging, March 15, 2006

THE REASONS WOMEN FACE RETIREMENT INCOME INSECURITY

The fundamental issues are these: women work fewer years, earn less, live longer and are likely to live alone in old age, which is highly correlated to poverty. Women must plan for a longer retirement with less income — the median income for women age 65 and older is only 57 percent of men in that age group. This should not come as a surprise — since the retirement system is based on what workers earn — so women are left with inadequate pensions and savings. The result is that women must rely too heavily on Social Security as an income source in retirement. Women, along with their male counterparts, tend also to lack basic financial knowledge, which is often the reason for making serious financial mistakes. Women need the best information available to ensure that they do not make financial mistakes; this information should be targeted to women as spouses and caregivers, as well as to women employees.

Family Responsibilities Relate to Working Fewer Years

Women continue to serve as their families' primary care givers for both children and older parents, and as a result, are more likely to work part-time in jobs without benefits or take time out of the workforce. The Social Security Administration finds that among new retired-worker beneficiaries, women average 13 years of zero earnings since age 22. This is on average 13 fewer years to earn a pension if one is even available; 13 fewer years to climb the ladder toward better jobs and better pay; and 13 fewer years to put money away through a defined contribution plan or IRA. Every time a career is interrupted, the ladder toward better jobs and better pay must be re-established when a woman rejoins the labor force. She loses not only time but often must start over after taking time off.

Other Economic Consequences of Family Caregiving

Since caring for the family is not recognized in this country as an economic contribution, women lose out by bearing the main share of this responsibility. Research shows that the economic consequence for single women who care for their elderly parents is a likelihood of life in poverty: caregivers are 2.5 times more likely than non-caregivers to live in poverty.[1]

For married women, a divorce or widowhood is a also threat to economic security. In 2003, 12.2 percent of men and 15.9 percent of women in their early 60s were divorced. With this trend expected to continue, there is not just a decline in a woman's standard of living, but the likely loss of future retirement benefits. For example, under a defined benefit pension plan, a married woman has a legal claim on her husband's benefit. With traditional pensions on the wane, and defined contribution plans on the rise, this safeguard is stripped away: married women currently have no legal right to control how 401(k) plan benefits are paid.[2]

Married women who rely on their spouse's benefits must be educated about the requirements of their spouse's retirement plans. There are a large number of inconsistencies among plans that dramatically affect widows. Women can find themselves falling through the cracks at the worst possible time in their lives. It is time for Congress to introduce a separate bill and fix this once and for all. Some of these "fixes" have been introduced again and again since fellow panelist, the Honorable Barbara Kennelly, first introduced her retirement bills in the House of Representatives.

Earning Power

Women have joined the labor force in record numbers, have many more opportunities and work in many different fields, but there is still a substantial pay difference between men and women. Women are paid less than men in almost *every* occupational classification for which data are available. Data through 2004 show full-time working women in the aggregate earn 77 cents for every dollar earned by a man.[3] At the same time that women began to increase their workforce participation, there was a trend toward greater out-of-pocket payment for both health benefits and for retirement savings plans such as 401(k)s and 403(b)s.

The figures on net worth tell the story: in 2001, married households had a median net worth of about $136,000, while households headed by single women had a net worth of about $29,500.[4]

Even when controlling for variables like position in the life cycle, education, inheritance and family earnings, the wealth gap remains.

Employee Benefits

Only 53 percent of women employees participate in an employer-sponsored pension plan.[5] Aside from lower earnings which means less access to plans, women are twice as likely to work part- time, and part-time workers are less likely to have retirement plans or they work at jobs that do not offer retirement plans. That said, if a woman does work for an employer with a tax deferred savings plan—such as a 401(k) or 403(b)—she is less likely than a man to contribute to it, largely because she earns less.

Reliance on Social Security

Social Security is the predominant source of retirement income for millions of older women. In fact, women make up 57 percent of adult beneficiaries.[6] For one in four older women, Social Security is the only source of income in their retirement. Without Social Security, the poverty rate for women would be significantly higher, increasing from about 12 percent to more than 50 percent.[7] The proportion of people aged 65 and older in poverty decreased from 35 percent in 1959 to 10 percent in 2003, the decline is mostly due to the support of Social Security. The most important thing that can be done for women is to strengthen the Social Security system to make sure that it continues to take women's lives into account and that it continues to meet the needs of low to moderate income workers.

Minority Women

Social Security is the only source of retirement income for 59 percent of single black women and 53 percent of single Hispanic women over age 65. The reasons why minority women fare poorly in retirement are lower earnings, employment patterns, caregiving responsibilities and marital status. WISER's report, *Minority Women and Retirement Income: Your Future Paycheck* documents the poverty rates: for single black women over age 65 it is 39.6 percent and for single Hispanic women it is 40.8 percent – twice the rate of white women. Any future reforms to the nation's retirement systems must consider the impact on low-income minority women.

Longevity

It is well established that women tend to live longer than men. The problem with living longer is that women's average income after the age of 65 is only about half that of men's. In fact, the median retirement income in 2004 for women was $12,080 compared to men's income of $21,102.[8]

With living longer comes the very real prospect of living alone and needing care. In 2000, only 40 percent of older women were married, compared to 74 percent of older men. Older women living alone are much more likely to be poor. Another well known fact is that the age 85 + group is expected to double over the next three decades — the group most likely to be living in poverty. Again, it is no surprise that after age 70, nursing home entry causes married women to lose one third of their wealth while single women lose about 60 percent of their wealth.

The numbers are daunting and the need for a discussion of long–term care as part of the financial discussion of retirement is long overdue. Many of the individuals who live to these older ages, particularly those who live after age 80, will need long-term care. Often when one member of a couple requires long-term care in a nursing home, it is likely that the survivor will be impoverished.

The demographics of older Americans points to the importance of women's retirement security:

- At 65 and older, there are 6.2 million more women than men.
- At ages 75 and older, there are 4 million more women than men.
- At 85 and older, there are 1.8 million more women than men. This amounts to 71 percent of the 85 and older population.[9]

Financial Knowledge

There is ample evidence that Americans lack financial knowledge, and that low financial knowledge is correlated to investing in an overly conservative way. This results in lower rates of return over time, and reduces the amount of savings set aside for retirement.

Women and men both suffer the consequences of being overly conservative in financial decisions. A recent study shows that, when controlling for age, income and educational attainment, women and men appear to make similar financial decisions.[10] Therefore, financial education for all Americans — women and men alike — is an ever-growing need that requires more resources to address.

At WISER, we know first-hand the gaps in financial knowledge among women. One of WISER's key initiatives is the program funded by the Administration on Aging—the National Women's Resource Center and Program on Women's Education for Retirement, also known as the POWERCenter. The Center's primary goal is to educate the most women we can possibly reach with information that can assist in retirement planning, and provide average and low- income women with the opportunity to take the first step toward controlling their financial futures. We have directly reached more than 25,000 women through our workshops and outreach with our publications. WISER's strength is providing women with core financial knowledge that encourages them to make retirement planning a priority in their lives. Women need to learn about their health and retirement benefits at work or the implication of the lack of such benefits, the financial implications of providing care for children, parents and spouses and the risks of longevity. Women are grateful for the information and sometimes just call and thank us for helping them avoid disaster. But this program needs to be replicated around the country and while at WISER we do what we can and work with many organizations, our funding is limited.

What Policymakers Can Do

As the distribution of wealth in the United States is so highly skewed — with a large percentage of total wealth held by a small percentage of the population, it is important for Congress to take steps that will benefit a larger number of moderate income workers. Many of the incentives in the retirement system are not being utilized by a majority of workers. In fact, the number of people who contribute the maximum to their 401(k) plans is barely 11 percent of all workers and the number who contribute to IRAs is even less.

It is important for policymakers to take several steps that will help women to access benefits and to mitigate the risks that prevent them from attaining greater retirement security.

Social Security

As the mainstay of support for women, the Social Security program has helped to protect many women from outright poverty in old age. Any future changes to the program should retain the income support features on which low and moderate income Americans rely most heavily. Social Security could be improved for women by:

- Providing credits for years devoted to care giving.
- Changing divorce benefits to make sense for two-earner families, individuals with time in and out of the labor force and to recognize earlier and more frequent divorce. The 10 year rule requirement should be changed to seven years.
- Changing widow benefits to make sense for a two-earner family.

Employment-Based System

Among improvements to the private employment-based retirement system, Congress should look to:

- Support and encourage the continued sponsorship of defined benefit pension plans or a more portable plan with the best features of the much maligned cash balance plans.
- Encourage annuities as an investment and distribution option in defined contribution plans and IRAs. This would address the need for basic spousal protections in 401(k) plans and rollover IRAs. While this is a complicated issue with a lot of contention among the players, annuities would provide the protection for spouses without regulating 401 (k)s in a way that employers would find objectionable.
- Encourage automatic enrollment and other pro-saving defaults in 401(k)-type defined contribution plans, with appropriate backstops to ensure that employers continue to have an incentive to increase participation by non-highly compensated workers.
- Analyze the coverage rules to identify possible opportunities to increase women's coverage.
- Expand, extend and simplify the Saver's Tax Credit to provide a financial incentive for moderate and lower income workers to save for retirement.
- Make sure that asset limits in means-tested programs do not penalize lower income workers who save for retirement.
- . Promote incentives for older workers to continue working and improve employment training and retraining programs to better serve older workers
- Address spiraling health care costs, including the cost of long-term care, recognizing that there can be simply no retirement security in the absence of health reforms.

Financial Education

In addition, policymakers can encourage better understanding of financial issues among all Americans. Policymakers should encourage employers and others to educate workers about retirement planning and saving and highlight the specific issues of importance to women.

PROPOSED SOLUTIONS: WHAT EMPLOYERS CAN DO

Employers can take several steps to help provide women with greater retirement security.

Social Security

Employers should support Social Security as an important means of filling the retirement income picture for their employees. Employers should support several specific changes that will retain Social Security's role as a critical income support system. I will outline these proposals shortly.

Retirement Benefits

Employers are important partners in the provision of retirement security. Employers should:

- Offer retirement programs appropriate to their industry and competitive environment. The best programs offer something for all eligible employees regardless of individual action.
- Tailor programs to work well even for those employees who do not plan well, and consider plan provisions such as auto-enrollment, balanced investment defaults and income as the automatic form of payout at retirement.
- Make it easy and financially attractive for employees to get their benefits as an income guaranteed for life, including a survivor option.
- Create options both for working longer and phasing into retirement. Working longer enables the accumulation of better benefits for retirement.
- Provide access to health benefits, at least to Medicare eligibility.

Financial Education

In addition, employers can be partners in the financial education process. Employers and policy - makers have an interest in education on the same issues. The critical information that should be targeted particularly to address women's issues includes:

- The importance of life decisions related to retirement benefits, such as when taking and leaving jobs, marrying and getting divorced.
- The need to hold onto retirement assets between jobs. Women are more likely to spend their lump-sum retirement distributions between jobs, because they have smaller balances in their accounts.
- Planning for contingencies such as widowhood and divorce.
- The effects of various types of insurance on retirement planning, such as long term care policies.

What Women Can Do: Five Important Steps Women Can Take

- Make retirement planning a priority.
- Learn as much as they can about their benefits on the job and their spouse's benefits.
- Educate themselves about their longevity risks as this is a serious issue.
- Estimate their needs and consider the impact of inflation.

- If possible, women need to save more and work longer.

IF WE DON'T ACT

If we look at various studies, it is clear that we will have a huge burden as a society. Some indicate that 75 percent of the baby boomers are not prepared for retirement; the average amount in 401(k)s for the group closest to retirement ages 55-64 is anywhere from $21,000 to $110,000 depending on the study. According to the most recent Federal Reserve Board study, the typical household account balance is $83,000, while the Survey of Consumer Finances reports a median of $60,000. These numbers are dramatic, because this is the group closest to retirement age.

Yet the solution we hear about most in the popular press is that boomers will continue to work. While this may sound like a good idea, circumstances may prevent work for some obvious reasons — no access to a job or bad health, or in the case of many women, providing care for a spouse, mother or a mother-in-law. These circumstances, sometimes referred to as negative shocks, may cause significant financial consequences.

A recent study by the Urban Institute illustrates a way to measure the financial impact of negative shocks. The paper reviews two 10-year periods for those aged 5 1-61 and for those aged 70 and older.[11] What's surprising is that 3/4ths of adults in the earlier group aged 5 1-61 experience one of these negative shocks:

- Three percent experience divorce.
- Ten percent experience widowhood.
- Forty–one percent experience major new medical conditions.
- Thirty-three percent experience health related work limitations.
- Nearly twenty percent experience job layoffs.

These events often threaten financial security at older ages, but it is especially problematic when they strike adults who may not have completed their retirement preparations.

CONCLUDING REMARKS

Despite the legal, social and economic gains made by American women in recent decades, economic insecurity remains a critical issue.

Women's work patterns and caregiving responsibilities will continue to place them at a significant disadvantage in our nation's retirement system. Moreover, the outcome of the current national debate about the future of Social Security and Medicare could have major implications for women's retirement security.

Women of all ages need your help, but the coming generations need it most. Our society is not prepared for the millions of women who will need long-term themselves after providing it for others. Your leadership on these issues is not just welcomed, but crucial if we as a nation are to alter the otherwise startling outlook faced by millions of women in this country.

Thank you for your time and consideration. I am pleased to respond to any questions Committee members have at this time.

REFERENCES

[1] Donato, Katharine and Wakabayashi, Chizuko: Women Caregivers are More Likely to Face Poverty, *Sallyport, Magazine of Rice University* Vol., 61 No.3. Spring 2005.

[2] Munnell, Alicia and Steven A. Sass: 401(k) Plans and Women: A "Good News/Bad News" Story. *Just the Facts on Retirement Issues*, Number 13. Center for Retirement Research at Boston College. January 2005.

[3] US Census Bureau: *Income, Poverty, and Health Insurance Coverage in the United States*: 2004, p.5. August 2005.

[4] Schmidt, Lucie and Purvi Sevak: *Gender, Marriage, and Asset Accumulation in the United States.* University of Michigan Retirement Research Center Working Paper WP 2005-109. December 2005.

[5] Beedon, Laurel and Ke Bin Wu: *Women Age 65 and Older: Their Sources of Income.* AARP Public Policy Institute. October 2005.

[6] Institute for Women's Policy Research: *Six Key Facts on Women and Social Security.* IWPR Fact Sheet #D462. May 2005.

[7] AARP: *Women and Social Security: What You Should Know.* Source: www.aarp.org/states/wv/wv-news/a-2004- 1 0-06-wv-wome.

[8] U.S. Census Bureau: Housing and Household Economic Statistics Division Revised January 13, 2006.

[9] He, Wan, Manisha Sengupta, Victoria A. Velkoff , and Kimberly A. DeBarros: U.S. Census Bureau, Current Population Reports, P23-209, *65+ in the United States: 2005*, U.S. Government Printing Office, Washington, DC, 2005.

[10] Papke, Leslie E: Individual Financial Decisions in Retirement Savings Plans: The Role of Participant-Direction. *Journal of Public Economics*, 88(1-2): 39-61.

[11] Johnson, Richard W., Gordon B.T. Mermin, Cori E. Ucello: *When the Nest Egg Cracks: Financial Consequences of Health Problems, Marital Status Changes, and Job Layoffs at Older Ages.* Urban Institute. January 2006.

In: Challenges Women Face in Retirement Security
Editor: Jean B. Larou, pp. 23-25

ISBN: 978-1-60741-747-7

Chapter 4

Testimony of Karyne Jones, President and Chief Executive Officer, the National Caucus and Center on Black Aged, Inc., before the Senate Special Committee on Aging, March 15, 2006, Dirksen Senate Office Building*

The Special Challenges of Women in Preparing for Financial Security in Retirement

The National Caucus and Center on Black Aged is pleased to testify before the Committee on the special challenges of women preparing for financial security in retirement. NCBA has a 36-year history of focusing our efforts on improving the quality of life for elderly low- income minorities in the country.

Retirement planning is important for everyone, but it is especially important and challenging for minority women. Minority women are less likely to work in jobs covered by pensions. Only 15 percent of Black and 8 percent of Hispanic older women received pension income in 2000. For those working today, 38 percent of Black women, 26 percent of Hispanic women, and 38 percent of Asian/Pacific Islander women are covered by a pension plan. This rate drops sharply when looking at part-time workers: 11 percent of Black women, 7 percent of Hispanic, and 10 percent of Asian/Pacific Islander women are covered by a pension plan.

Despite the overall decline in poverty rates among older Americans during the last several decades, many older women remain poor. Approximately, 12.4 percent of women age 65 and older are poor compared to 7 percent of the men in this age group, and the likelihood of a woman being poor in retirement increases with age. The poverty rate for single black women over age 65 is 41.5 percent, and for single Hispanic women it is 49.2 percent twice the rate of white women. The reality is that many women rely on Social Security as their primary source of income in retirement. In fact, Social Security is the only source of

* This is an edited, reformatted and augmented version of testimony before the United States Senate Special Committee on Aging, March 15, 2006.

retirement income for 45 percent of unmarried black women and 46% of unmarried Hispanic women over age 65. The problem is that Social Security was not designed to be a retiree's sole source of support, but instead was meant to provide only a bare minimum of protection.

We understand the current push for Americans to save. However, women's lower earnings often leave them with few resources to invest. Women usually have little or no money left to save for retirement after paying their bills. Furthermore, the current generation of elderly women of all races has little in the way of savings and investments for their retirement. In fact, half of all unmarried older women have less than $1,278 a year in asset income, or only about $106 a month.

Women should be saving more money than men because on average they live about 4 more years than men, and will need money to support themselves. And, they are also more likely to have higher expenses for health care and prescription drugs. Unfortunately, women's lower average earnings and more time spent out of the workforce for care giving make it difficult for many of them to save the amounts needed for retirement much less have the resources to make catch-up contributions.

Minority populations are also living longer, and by the year 2050, experts are projecting that there will be at least five times more minority women and men aged 65 and older, and about thirteen times more who are aged 85 and older. Minority women will comprise a larger percentage of the older population in the years ahead. Also, for minority women with limited work histories or who have lived on the margin economically, the retirement picture looks particularly bleak. For example, minority women who might have worked in domestic capacity or as a day laborer probably did not earn enough money to contribute to personal savings account and certainly not a pension plan.

Women overall have made many financial improvements over the past 25 years, and some are finding reason for optimism. A recent survey of African American women on behalf of the Fannie Mae Foundation suggests that while half of African American women are struggling to make ends meet, they are optimistic that their financial situation will improve over the next year.

Younger minority women who spend many years in the labor force and in higher-paid jobs will be the most likely to be able to save and plan for a financially secure old age. Most women, regardless of race or ethnicity, will need to plan carefully in order to deal with the risk of outliving their assets, and to manage carefully to cover the high costs of health care and longer life spans. NCBA has focused our attention on educating young people on preparing for old age in hopes of addressing

The harsh reality remains that, as long as most minority women earn less money than other women and men, and have fewer opportunities to save, they will have less retirement income and face the highest risks of poverty in old age.

POLICY REFORMS

Many improvements can be made by policymakers to provide low-income minority women with greater retirement security. Some of the pension reform proposals currently under consideration by lawmakers that could enhance women's retirement security include: increasing pension coverage for lower-wage, part-time and temporary workers, increasing survivor benefits, making pension division upon divorce more equitable for women, and giving women credit for care giving.

As a society, we have an obligation to provide older women with the opportunity to live out their later years with adequate resources that will lead to a dignified retirement. However, as long as most minority women earn less money than other women and men, and have fewer opportunities to save, they will have less retirement income and face the highest risks of poverty in old age. In conclusion, increasing survivor benefits, making pension division upon divorce more equitable for women, and giving women credit for care giving are just a few ways to offer women some relief during the retirement years.

In: Challenges Women Face in Retirement Security
Editor: Jean B. Larou, pp. 27-29
ISBN: 978-1-60741-747-7

Chapter 5

SENATE SPECIAL COMMITTEE ON AGING, BRIDGING THE GENDER GAP: ELIMINATING RETIREMENT INCOME DISPARITY FOR WOMEN, TESTIMONY OF BARBARA KENNELLY, PRESIDENT, NATIONAL COMMITTEE TO PRESERVE SOCIAL SECURITY AND MEDICARE, MARCH 15, 2006*

Mr. Chairman and Ranking Member Kohl:

Thank you so much for inviting me to speak to you on the important issue of women's financial security in retirement. I greatly appreciate this opportunity.

The National Committee to Preserve Social Security and Medicare is a grassroots advocacy organization representing 4.6 million members and supporters. As our name indicates, our primary mission is the preservation of Social Security and Medicare, because these programs are the lynchpin of senior's retirement security. But we also care a great deal about other issues that affect the quality of life of America's retirees.

The question of women's retirement security is, of course, a critical one as our nation looks to the future. The main reason is that we women live *forever*. We also tend to reach retirement age with fewer resources than men. That means we have less money that must be stretched out over a longer period of time.

As you know, retirement used to be thought of as a three-legged stool, with Social Security, employer-sponsored pensions, and personal savings making up relatively equal legs. Over time, however, it's become increasingly clear that the three-legged stool has become more like a bar stool, with Social Security forming the central pillar upon which retirement rests. This problem is not unique to women – men are also relying increasingly on Social Security in retirement. But the problem is particularly acute for women because of the combination of longer life expectancies and fewer resources.

Because other witnesses will discuss pensions and personal savings, I will concentrate on what is increasingly becoming the central pillar of retirement – Social Security.

---

* This is an edited, reformatted and augmented version of Testimony before the United States Senate Special Committee on Aging, March 15, 2006

According to the Social Security Administration, women reaching age 65 in 2004 are expected to live, on average, an additional 20 years compared with 17 years for men. Women represent 58% of all Social Security beneficiaries age 62 and older, and approximately 70% of all beneficiaries age 85 and older.

For all the reasons your other panelists have mentioned, women are much more heavily reliant on Social Security than men are. Social Security is the only source of retirement income for 29% of unmarried elderly women. Those women who have other income are still highly dependent on Social Security. For unmarried women over age 65, Social Security comprises 52% of their total income, compared with 38% for unmarried elderly men, and 35% for elderly couples. Were it not for Social Security, more than two-thirds of elderly women would live in poverty.

Social Security has two protections that are particularly important to women. First, the benefit lasts as long as we live, so there's no risk of outliving our assets. Second, the program's Cost of Living Adjustment helps protect against the ravages of inflation. This is a feature that does not exist in most other sources of retirement income, and it is particularly critical for women because of their longevity.

While we disagreed with the President on his proposal to divert payroll taxes into private accounts, we absolutely agree on the need to strengthen the program's long-term solvency, particularly as we stand on the eve of baby boomer retirements. According to projections by the Census Bureau, over 7,900 people a day – or 330 an hour – will turn age 60 during 2006 alone. It is absolutely crucial that our nation be prepared for this wave of seniors.

One issue that often comes up during discussions of Social Security's solvency is the question of raising the retirement age. As you know, it is currently 67 for those born in 1960 or later. Raising the retirement age is perceived to address two key problems – the solvency of retiree programs such as Social Security and our economy's need for a sufficiently large workforce. Yet there is a significant disconnect between older worker's expectations and reality where staying in the workforce is concerned. Surveys, including one done recently by AARP, show that more than two-thirds of today's older workers, and 80% of baby boomers, plan to work in retirement. But the reality is that over half of Social Security beneficiaries retire at age 62 and almost 80% are retired by age 65.

The reasons for this are varied. In many cases, workers who expected to keep working into retirement find that their health deteriorates to the point where they cannot continue. In other cases, they lose long-held jobs through no fault of their own and then have difficulty finding other employment. According to a recent study by the Congressional Research Service, only 60% of men and 55% of women who lost their jobs at 55 years of age were employed two years later. Finally, there are those whose employers offer incentives for early retirement, and when the employees take the offer they often find it difficult to re-enter the workforce.

When employers are surveyed, they seem to acknowledge the problem, but have done very little to address it. Nationwide, over 40% of the U.S. workforce is estimated to be eligible to retire over the next 5 years, and over one-half of employers believe this will lead to a workforce shortage. Yet recent surveys show only 14% of employers have any kind of formal program to retain or attract older workers.

My point is that keeping older workers employed is not as simple as raising the retirement age. Much work must be done to educate employers on the value of an older workforce. And incentives must be provided to help alleviate the costs of retaining longer tenured workers. On the employee side, we must identify and remove the disincentives to continued work that exist today.

While some studies show that the cost difference between employing workers aged 50 and older and younger workers is only 1% to 3%, the cost of employing older workers is a pervasive theme in employer surveys. Not only are older workers likely to have higher salaries because of their long service with the employer, but the cost of their healthcare and pension benefits is also higher than that of younger workers. While the turnover costs of replacing any experienced worker can reach 50% of the worker's salary, this expense can seem small when compared to the higher overall compensation cost. These concerns clearly must be addressed if we expect employers to accommodate the needs of older workers.

On the employee side, according to a recent survey by Towers Perrin, the top three factors identified by workers aged 50 or older as keys to their decision to continue working for a company are the availability of a competitive healthcare package, the ability to continue participating in the retirement plan, and the ability to strike a balance between work and home.

Yet, according to the Bureau of Labor Statistics, only 11 percent of workers participate in a formal flexible work program, only 27 percent of part-time workers have access to retirement benefits, and only 22 percent of part-time workers have access to health benefits. The disconnect between the needs and expectations of older workers and their employers cannot be more obvious.

That is why I find proposals such as Senator Kohl's Older Worker Opportunity Act a tremendous step in the right direction. His bill focuses on the issues that are key to both employers and older workers, in an effort to address the concerns of both partners in the employment equation. His bill acknowledges the desire of older workers to have a better balance between work and their home life by encouraging employers to offer part-time work. And he addresses the concerns expressed by both workers and their employers by helping subsidize the cost of allowing these part-time older workers to continue receiving health benefits and to continue participating in company pension plans.

The key mechanism for accomplishing these goals in S.1826 is through the tax code. By providing a tax benefit for companies who employ older workers while allowing them to work part time, keep their health care coverage and participate in the company retirement plan, I believe this legislation could go a long way toward paving the way for significant increases in older worker employment.

Mr. Chairman, as our society ages, the need to keep older workers employed will become a much higher priority for both workers and employers. Now is the time to explore the impediments for senior employment and begin removing them. This hearing in and of itself is an important step in highlighting the problem, and I believe bills such as the Older Worker Opportunity Act are good first steps toward that goal.

Thank you again for inviting me to join you this morning.

In: Challenges Women Face in Retirement Security
Editor: Jean B. Larou, pp. 31-32
ISBN: 978-1-60741-747-7

Chapter 6

STATEMENT OF SENATOR HERB KOHL – MARCH 15, 2006, "BRIDGING THE GENDER GAP: ELIMINATING RETIREMENT INCOME DISPARITY FOR WOMEN"*

Thank you, Mr. Chairman, for holding this important hearing. As we will hear today, women tend to receive less income during their retirement years than men—in fact, they get only about 53 percent of what men receive. The poverty rate for single women of retirement age is a staggering *17 percent*. That is simply unacceptable.

Retirement security is often thought of as a "three-legged stool"—Social Security, employer pensions, and private saving. But it's clear that for too many women facing retirement, that stool is shaky. We must strengthen all three legs, and also promote a fourth leg—the opportunity to continue working past traditional retirement age for those who need to do so.

Social Security is the foundation of retirement security for everyone, especially women. In fact, it is the *only* source of income for over one-quarter of single elderly women. Social Security provides a guaranteed benefit—even more important now that individuals are bearing more risk in defined contribution plans. Furthermore, Social Security benefits are protected from inflation and guaranteed to last a lifetime; this is especially important for women, who on average live about 5 years longer than men. And finally, Social Security is progressive—it replaces a larger share of earnings for low-earners, and women tend to earn less than men. Social Security is a lifesaver for many women, and we must protect and strengthen it.

But because Social Security was never meant to be the sole support after retirement, we must also strengthen employer pensions and private saving. Women are more likely to work part-time and therefore are less likely to be covered by a pension plan. Women are also increasingly at risk of outliving their savings, because unlike traditional pensions, few defined contribution plans offer to pay out benefits as an annuity—an income stream that is guaranteed to last a lifetime.

---

* This is an edited, reformatted and augmented version of statment before the United States Senate on March 15, 2006

We should encourage 40 1(k) plans to offer an annuity payout, and encourage participants to choose this option. In addition, we should extend and expand the Saver's Credit so we can help lower-income people, many of whom are women, better save for retirement.

Even with such improvements, many baby boomers will choose to work longer. Some will work to stay healthy and productive, and some will work because they need to build more savings for a comfortable retirement. This new "fourth leg" of the retirement stool—continued work past traditional retirement age—will be especially important for women, who tend to live longer than men.

Yet for several reasons, older women are less likely to participate in the labor force today, making saving for retirement more difficult. First, women are more likely to seek part-time and flexible work schedules—and companies are less likely to provide pension plans for part-time workers. Second, many are responsible for caring for elderly or disabled relatives. Caregiving reduces their earnings, Social Security benefits, and pension benefits—on average, a total loss of $659,139 over a lifetime.

I have introduced legislation that would address these barriers and expand the time older workers have to work, save, and secure a more comfortable retirement. The bill would provide tax incentives for businesses to hire and retain older workers, offer them part-time and flextime opportunities, and include them in the company's pension and health insurance plans. It also seeks to ease the burden on caregivers – who more often tend to be women—by giving a tax credit to workers for the care of their senior family members.

We face an enormous challenge, but if we work together for common sense reform and encourage businesses to adopt best practices, we can ensure that all four legs of the retirement stool—including the opportunity to work—stand firm for women. I look forward to continuing that effort in our dialogue today.

In: Challenges Women Face in Retirement Security
Editor: Jean B. Larou, pp. 33-34
ISBN: 978-1-60741-747-7

Chapter 7

STATEMENT OF CHAIRMAN GORDON H. SMITH, U.S. SENATE SPECIAL COMMITTEE ON AGING, "BRIDGING THE GENDER GAP: ELIMINATING RETIREMENT INCOME DISPARITY FOR WOMEN", MARCH 15, 2006*

Good morning, and thank you all for coming.

We're here today to discuss a topic of growing concern in America—women and retirement security. We will explore reasons why there is a gap in retirement income between men and women, the factors behind why women face greater financial risk and ways to assist women in planning for retirement.

Preparing for retirement and achieving financial security are daunting tasks for all Americans to be sure; however, women face many unique challenges. For example, women still perform the primary caretaker role in our society. As a result, many women spend significant periods of time out of the workforce raising children or taking care of elderly parents, significantly diluting their earning power.

Women also are more likely to work part-time or work in industries where employers are less likely to offer retirement benefits.

And women generally earn less than men. In 2004, women earned 77 cents for every dollar earned by men.

All of these factors have a significant impact on what women receive from Social Security and pensions, as well as what they are able accumulate through personal savings. The bottom line is it's harder to accumulate retirement income when you're making less money—and working for fewer years.

As a result, women receive significantly less income during retirement than men. This is true for all three legs of the retirement income stool—Social Security, pensions and savings.

In 2004, the median annual income of women over the age of 65 was $12,000. Men on the other hand had income of about $21,000. Although this figure is extremely low for men as well, women received almost half of what men collected in retirement.

---

* This is an edited, reformatted and augmented version of a statement before the United States Senate Special Committee on Aging, March 15, 2006

This income gap is further exacerbated by the fact that women generally live longer than men—and therefore need to stretch their income over a longer period of time.

Equally disturbing is the high rate of poverty among older women. Of the 3.5 million Americans over the age of 65 who were in poverty in 2004, about 70 percent were women.

Due to many factors, including high divorce rates and the fact that women generally live longer, many women will spend a portion of their retirement years without a spouse or significant other. However, living alone can have serious consequences on one's financial security.

In 2004, the poverty rate for married women over the age of 65 was 4.4 percent. For unmarried women, the poverty rate was 17.4 percent – almost four times higher. And the rate is much higher for single black and Hispanic women.

I have spent a great deal of time over the last year examining the issue of retirement savings and security. Last June, I introduced a bi-partisan bill with Senator Kent Conrad of North Dakota dealing with this issue. Although the bill is aimed at increasing savings and ensuring greater financial security in retirement for all Americans, many of the proposals address the unique challenges that women face.

For example, America's savings rate for both men and women can best be described as dismal. Our national personal-savings rate had declined dramatically over the last two decades and today is less than zero.

My bill encourages employers to adopt automatic enrollment in 401(k) plans, a simple idea that has been shown to increase participation significantly – especially among low and moderate income individuals. A study of employees who earn less than $20,000 showed 401(k) participation rates increased from 13 percent to 80 percent when the employees were automatically enrolled, an amazing increase for such a simple change.

My proposed legislation also expands the Saver's Credit, which is a tax credit for certain low and moderate-income individuals who contribute to workplace retirement plans and IRAs. The Saver's Credit has been hugely successful in encouraging savings and is used by more than five million Americans each year. Unfortunately it is set to expire this year. My bill remedies this by extending the credit through 2010 so those who most need to save for the future are encouraged to do so.

Another key component provides incentives for lifetime payments. Since women generally live longer than men, they must be particularly concerned with protecting against the risk of exhausting their retirement income. Life annuities help ensure that older Americans will not outlive their retirement savings, adding stability and security in our retirement years.

Although these are good first steps, more needs to be done. I am currently developing legislation with the specific goal of narrowing the retirement income gap between men and women. To assist in drafting this bill, I have organized a "kitchen cabinet" of retirement experts who are concerned with the financial security of women. This group includes benefits attorneys, financial services companies, advocacy groups and organizations representing employers. My hope is that by bringing together this broad coalition, we'll be able to develop bi-partisan solutions to this very challenging problem.

Lastly, I'd like to thank our witnesses who join us this morning. I am eagerly anticipating your testimony and look forward to a productive dialog on ways we can begin to eliminate the retirement income gap problem.

With that, I'll turn to my colleague Senator Kohl for his opening remarks.

In: Challenges Women Face in Retirement Security
Editor: Jean B. Larou, pp. 35-48
ISBN: 978-1-60741-747-7

Chapter 8

WRITTEN STATEMENT FOR THE U.S. SENATE SPECIAL COMMITTEE ON AGING, HEARING ON BRIDGING THE GENDER GAP: ELIMINATING RETIREMENT INCOME DISPARITY FOR WOMEN, MARCH 15, 2006, "GENDER DISPARITIES IN RETIREMENT SECURITY"*†

Jack VanDerhei
Temple University and Research Director of the Employee Benefit Research Institute Fellows Program

INTRODUCTION

Although the Social Security retirement benefit program was put in place more than seven decades ago and the Employee Retirement Income Security Act (ERISA) was enacted more than three decades ago, it appears there will still be substantial numbers of future retirees who will struggle with retirement security. One recent study by the Employee Benefit Research Institute (EBRI)[1] found that American retirees will have at least $45 billion less in retirement income in 2030 than what they will need to cover basic expenditures and any expense associated with an episode of care in a nursing home or from a home health care provider. The aggregate deficit in retiree income during the decade ending 2030 will be at least $400 billion.

* The views expressed in this statement are solely those of Dallas L. Salisbury and should not be attributed to the Employee Benefit Research Institute (EBRI), the EBRI Education and Research Fund, any of its programs, officers, trustees, sponsors, or other staff. The Employee Benefit Research Institute is a nonprofit, nonpartisan, education and research organization established in Washington, DC in 1978. The testimony draws heavily from research publications of the Employee Benefit Research Institute, but any errors or misinterpretations are those of the witness.

† This is an edited, reformatted and augmented version of a written statement to the United States Senate Special Committee on Aging, March 15, 2006

While these numbers are troubling in aggregate, drilling down to see what the potential consequences of today's programs might be for certain segments of the retiree population in the future, especially single females, shows that achieving retirement security on a nearly universal basis will be a particularly daunting challenge.

This testimony begins by summarizing the sources of current retiree income, including Social Security and employment-based retirement plans, and then reviewing the current literature with respect to gender disparities in the percentage of workers with an employment-based retirement plan, the participation rates of those eligible to participate in a plan, and the contribution levels for those who have a plan allowing a contribution. The impact of the continuing evolution from defined benefit (pension) to defined contribution (401(k)-type) plans among private plan sponsors on future retirees' sources of income is demonstrated. This evolution transfers longevity risk to future retirees— and may have a disproportionate impact on women.

The last section of the testimony ties all of this together by showing the results of a simulation model that projects whether individuals will have sufficient money in retirement to pay for basic expenses plus the potential costs of long-term health care costs not typically covered by health insurance. The additional amounts needed to be saved to provide a specified level of retirement security are generated to show the values needed by birth cohorts, income quartiles, and gender.

OVERVIEW OF GENDER DISPARITIES IN CURRENT RETIREE INCOME SOURCES

Social Security

Based on numbers published by the Social Security Administration,[2] at the end of 2003, women's average monthly Social Security retirement benefit was $798, compared with $1,039 for their male counterparts. Given the gender-neutral calculation of retirement benefits[3] under Social Security, this disparity is largely due to the differences in average earnings prior to retirement[4] and the number of years the individual worked prior to receiving benefits. However, the current calculation method used for most workers provides that the full disparity between earnings and number of years worked prior to retirement is mitigated to a certain extent:

- The value of the worker's career earnings used to calculate the monthly benefits for most workers ignores any earnings greater than the maximum taxable wage base in that year. For example, in 2006 any earnings greater than $94,200 would be not be subject to Social Security payroll tax and thus would not be used in calculating the Social Security benefits for the individual.
- The value of the worker's career earnings used to calculate the monthly benefits for most workers only uses the 35 highest indexed values. This may be useful to mitigating the gender gap that otherwise would exist in two ways. First, the amount of earnings (below the maximum taxable wage base) is indexed for the increase in average national wages between the time of the earnings and the time the individual

reaches age 60. As a result, if a worker leaves the work force early (perhaps to take care of children or an aged parent), the previous earnings will not be artificially lowered due to overall wage growth in the country. Secondly, the calculation process typically allows several years of low (or zero) wage years to be ignored. For example, an individual entering the work force at age 21 and retiring at 65 could have left the work force for as many as nine full years without being penalized with respect to this calculation.

- The formula used to convert the workers' average indexed earnings to a monthly retirement benefit is heavily skewed toward lower-income workers. For example, if 2006 is the year in which the worker is first eligible for benefits, his or her initial monthly benefit at normal retirement age would be equal to the sum of:

  - 90 percent of the first $656 of average indexed monthly earnings, plus
  - 32 percent of the next $3,299 of average indexed monthly earnings, plus
  - 15 percent of any average indexed monthly earnings in excess of $3,955.

- In addition to retirement benefits based directly on one's own working history, an additional benefit may be available equal to 50 percent of the spouse's benefit less the benefit the worker would have been entitled to based on his or her own earnings.

Social Security plays a much larger role in total income for unmarried women over age 62 than for their male counterparts. Based on EBRI estimates from the March 2005 Current Population Survey (CPS), Social Security represents an average of 65.5 percent of total income for unmarried females over age 62 but only 56.1 percent for unmarried males over age 62. As seen in figure 1, this is largely a function of income—when results are reported by income quartile, these differences decrease significantly. For individuals in the first (lowest) income quartile (total income of $9,199 or less), Social Security represents an average of 79 percent of total income for women versus 75 percent for men. This number decreases significantly for both genders in the fourth (highest) quartile (total income of $61,398 or more): Social Security represents an average of 26.8 percent of total income for males and 27.6 percent for females.

Private Pensions

Based on EBRI estimates from the March 2005 CPS, 34.6 percent of those age 65 or older had pension income in 2004.[5] The mean amount was $13,951 and the median was $9,600. Among males 44.7 percent had pension income, as opposed to 27.0 percent for females. The mean amount for males was $17,175 while females averaged only $10,035. There was an even larger disparity in the median amounts: $12,012 for males and $6,600 for females.

Gender Distribution of Total Income Quartiles

	Male	Female
1st (lowest) Income Quartile	21.6%	78.4%
2nd	22.2%	77.8%
3rd	24.8%	75.2%
4th (highest) Income Quartile	40.2%	59.8%

Percentage of Total Income Social Security Represents, by Total Income Quartiles

	Mean	5th	25th	Median	75th	95th
All						
Total	63.2%	0.0%	32.7%	72.6%	100.0%	100.0%
Male	56.1%	0.0%	22.5%	55.9%	99.2%	100.0%
Female	65.5%	0.0%	37.1%	79.0%	100.0%	100.0%
First Quartile						
Total	78.3%	0.0%	79.1%	100.0%	100.0%	100.0%
Male	75.4%	0.0%	57.4%	100.0%	100.0%	100.0%
Female	79.0%	0.0%	83.8%	99.9%	100.0%	100.0%
Second Quartile						
Total	86.8%	23.5%	83.9%	99.7%	100.0%	100.0%
Male	84.9%	0.0%	83.9%	99.9%	100.0%	100.0%
Female	87.3%	34.5%	83.8%	99.6%	100.0%	100.0%
Third Quartile						
Total	62.9%	0.0%	47.3%	65.8%	86.5%	100.0%
Male	64.0%	0.0%	49.2%	66.0%	91.2%	100.0%
Female	62.6%	0.0%	46.7%	65.7%	85.3%	100.0%
Fourth Quartile						
Total	27.3%	0.0%	4.7%	26.8%	42.8%	64.2%
Male	26.8%	0.0%	6.1%	25.8%	43.2%	62.0%
Female	27.6%	0.0%	3.1%	27.1%	42.6%	65.2%

Source: EBRI estimates from the March 2005 Current Population Survey.

Figure 1. Importance of Social Security for Unmarried Individuals Age 62 and Older, 2003.

Gender Disparities in Retirement Program Participation among Current Workers

Although there is a substantial amount of gender disparity among those already age 65 with respect to receiving pension income, it appears this disparity will decrease sharply and for some worker types will actually reverse. As a case in point, Copeland[6] analyzes 2004 employment-based participation levels from the March 2005 CPS and finds that among the 152.7 million Americans who worked in 2004, 81.2 million worked for an employer or union that sponsored a pension or retirement plan, and 63.9 million participated in the plan. This translates into a sponsorship rate (the percentage of workers working for an employer or union that sponsored a plan) of 53.2 percent (52.3 percent for males and 54.2 percent for females) and a participation level (fraction of the workforce who participates in a plan regardless of eligibility) of 41.9 percent (42.5 percent for males and 41.2 percent for females). However, this measure of the work force contains the unincorporated self-employed and those typically with a looser connection to the work force—individuals under age 21 and older than age 64. Therefore, a different measure of the work force is examined: wage and salary workers ages 21–64, representing individuals who have a stronger connection to the work force and work for someone else. For this group, the sponsorship rate increases to 59.5

percent (59.0 percent for males and 60.1 percent for females) and the portion participating increases to 48.3 percent (49.4 percent for males and 47.2 percent for females). When separating these wage and salary workers into the public and private sectors, the percentages participating differ significantly. Slightly less than 76 percent (79.9 percent for males and 72.8 percent for females) of the public-sector workers participated in an employment-based retirement plan, compared with 43.0 percent (44.7 percent for males and 41.0 percent for females) of the private-sector workers.

A more restrictive definition of the work force, which more closely resembles the types of workers who generally must be covered by ERISA for a retirement plan offered by a private-sector employer or union, is the work force of full-time, full-year wage and salary workers ages 21–64. Approximately 57 percent (55.4 percent for males and 58.2 percent for females) of these workers participated in a retirement plan.

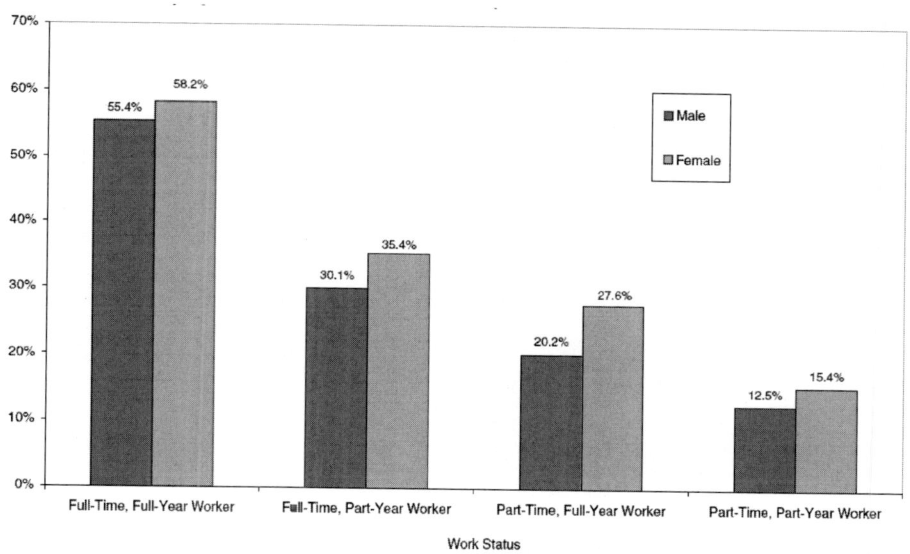

Source: Employee Benefit Research Institute estimates from 2005 March Current Population Survey.

Figure 2. Percentage of Wage and Salary Workers Ages 21–64 Who Participated in an Employment-Based Retirement Plan, by Work Status and Gender, 2004.

These gaps were significantly larger in the late 1980s. For example, in 1987, 40.7 percent of female wage and salary workers ages 21-64 participated in an employment-based retirement plan compared with 51.0 percent for males. The gap decreased from just over 10 percentage points to under 4 percentage points. Furthermore, while all female wage and salary workers ages 21–64 were found to participate in a retirement plan at a lower level than males did, the percentage of full-time, full-year female workers who participated in a plan was higher than for males. In fact, across all of the worker status categories, females were more likely to participate in a retirement plan than males (figure 2). Furthermore, when examining the participation by earnings level, the proportion of females participating in a plan was also higher than it was for males (figure3). Consequently, it appears that females' lower probability of participation in the aggregate was a result of female workers' overall lower earnings and/or lower rates of full-time work in comparison with males (figure 4).

Figure 5 shows the average employee contribution rate to salary reduction plans for nonagricultural wage and salary workers age 16 and over. On average, males contributed approximately 0.3 percentage points of compensation more than females in 1993. This difference decreased to approximately 0.1 percentage points of compensation in 1998 before increasing to 0.4 percentage points in 2003. It appears much of this differential is due to the propensity of those with larger incomes to contribute a larger percentage of compensation.

In a similar fashion, Copeland[7] shows the participation rate for salary reduction plans among those eligible is higher for males (84.3 percent) than females (79.1 percent). Again, these differences can be explained in large part by the gender income disparities.

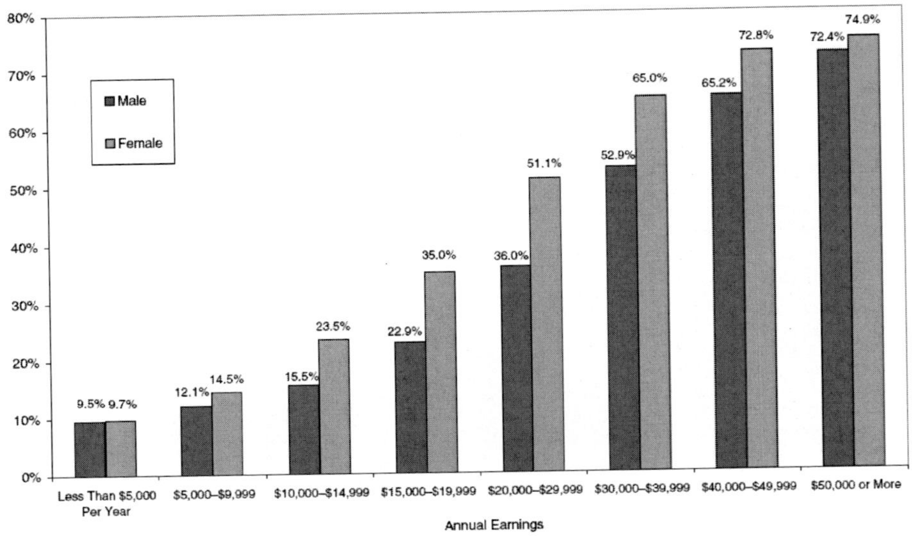

Source: Employee Benefit Research Institute estimates from 2005 March Current Population Survey.

Figure 3. Percentage of Wage and Salary Workers Ages 21–64 Who Participated in an Employment-Based Retirement Plan, by Annual Earnings and Gender, 2004.

	Overall	Men	Women
Annual Earnings			
Less than $5,000	12.1%	9.6%	14.9%
$5,000–$9,999	8.2%	6.0%	10.5%
$10,000–$14,999	8.8%	7.2%	10.7%
$15,000–$19,999	8.5%	7.5%	9.6%
$20,000–$29,999	17.0%	15.6%	18.5%
$30,000–$39,999	14.0%	14.1%	13.8%
$40,000–$49,999	9.6%	10.7%	8.4%
$50,000 or more	21.9%	29.3%	13.6%
Work Status			
Full-time, full-year	66.6%	73.6%	58.8%
Full-time, part-year	13.1%	13.2%	12.9%
Part-time, full-year	10.2%	6.2%	14.7%
Part-time, part-year	10.1%	7.0%	13.6%

Source: EBRI estimates from the March 2005 Current Population Survey.

Figure 4. Distribution of Workers, by Earnings and Work Status, by Gender.

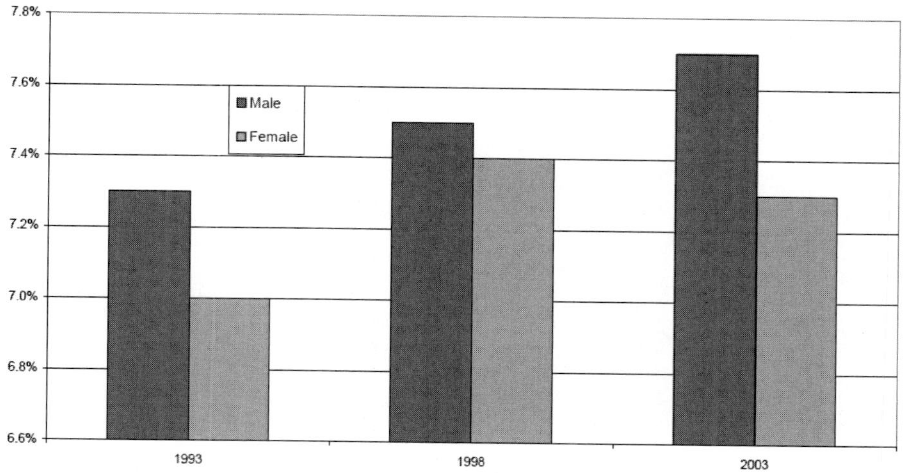

Source: Employee Benefit Research Institute estimates of the April 1993 Current Population Survey employee benefit supplement and the 1996 and 2001 Panel of the Survey of Income and Program Participation Topical Module 7.

Figure 5. Average Employee Contribution Rate to Salary Reduction Plans, Nonagricultural Wage and Salary Workers Age 16 and Over.

INCREASING IMPORTANCE OF INDIVIDUAL ACCOUNT PLANS FOR FUTURE RETIREMENT INCOME SECURITY

The increasing importance of this shift from defined benefit to defined contribution retirement plans can be seen in figures 6 and 7. Figure 6 provides the composition of estimated retirement wealth for males at Social Security normal retirement age, by birth cohort. Similar figures for females are provided in figure 7. It is readily apparent from these graphs that both genders have an appreciable drop in the percentage of private retirement income that is attributable to defined benefit plans (other than cash balance). Females start with a slightly higher defined benefit concentration than men (49.7 percent vs. 39.0 percent for the 1936 cohort), and the difference remains fairly constant over time (37.2 percent vs. 26.4 percent for the 1964 cohort).

These results show a clear increase in the income retirees will receive that will have to be managed by the retiree. This makes the risk of longevity more central to retirees' expenditure decisions. Therefore, they will have to understand that life expectancies are merely averages, and that wide variation beyond the average is possible. Moreover, as the percentage of overall retirement income derived from defined benefit plans decreases, females desiring longevity insurance in the form of an annuity will face the disadvantage of having to purchase products priced using gender-distinct mortality tables instead of the implicit gender-neutral nature of the defined benefit annuity structure. Given the longer life expectancies for females at retirement age, this can amount to an appreciable decrease in retirement income.[8]

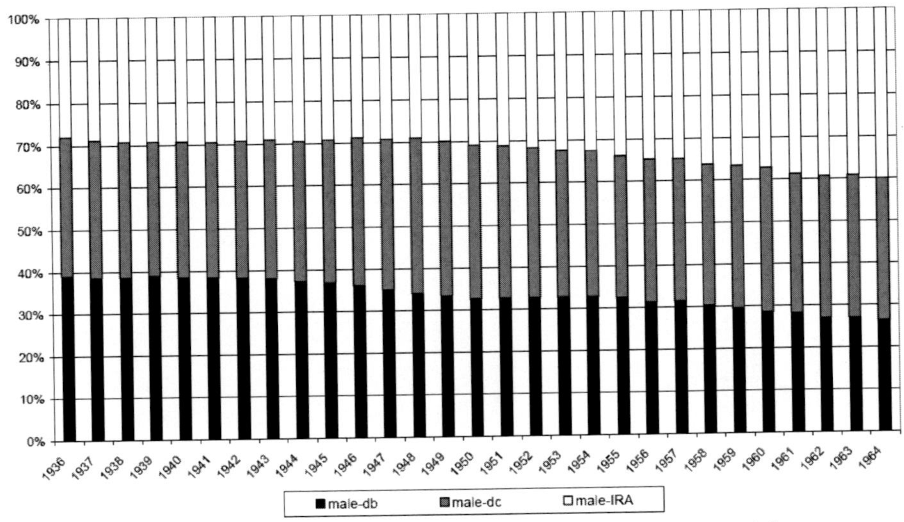

Source: Employee Benefit Research Institute, Retirement Income Projection Model.

Figure 6. Composition of Estimated Retirement Wealth for Males at Social Security Normal Retirement Age Under Baseline Assumptions, by Birth Cohort.

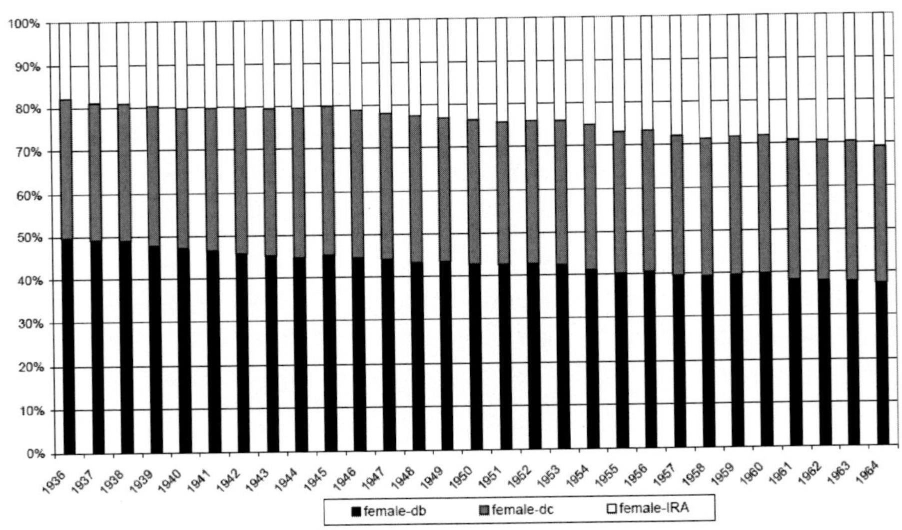

Source: Employee Benefit Research Institute, Retirement Income Projection Model.

Figure 7. Composition of Estimated Retirement Wealth for Males at Social Security Normal Retirement Age Under Baseline Assumptions, by Birth Cohort.

RETIREMENT INCOME ADEQUACY

While the previous material documented the component parts of the accumulation process, the real question from a public policy perspective may be whether current and future retirees will be able to afford an adequate standard of living in retirement. Significant work has been done by EBRI and others to evaluate how much workers will need in order to have the same after-tax and after-savings amount for consumption in retirement that they enjoyed prior to retirement.[9] Although this may be desirable from the standpoint of financial planning, it sets a goal that may be unrealistically high for many segments of the population. Another standard is used in this analysis to assess the current state of the retirement system.

Instead of attempting to determine what percentage of the population will be able to attain a specified replacement ratio,[10] this analysis attempts to model what percentage of retirees will have sufficient retirement wealth to pay for a basket of non-luxury goods in retirement for the remainder of their simulated life-paths.[11] The expenditures used in the model for the elderly consist of two components—deterministic (unchanging) and stochastic (variable) expense assumptions. The deterministic expenses include those expenses that the elderly incur from a basic need or want of daily life, while the stochastic expenses in this model are exclusively health-event related—e.g., an admission to a nursing home or the commencement of an episode of home health care—that occur only for a portion, if ever, during retirement, not on an annual basis.

Deterministic Retirement Expense Assumptions

The deterministic expenses are broken down into seven categories—food, apparel and services (dry cleaning, haircuts), transportation, entertainment, reading and education, housing, and basic health expenditures. Each of these expenses is estimated for the elderly (age 65 or older) by family size (single or couple) and family income (less than $15,000, $15,000 to $29,999, and $30,000, or more in 2002 dollars) of the family/individual.

The estimates are derived from the 2000 Consumer Expenditure Survey (CES) conducted by the Bureau of Labor Statistics of the U.S. Department of Labor. The survey targets the total noninstitutionalized population (urban and rural) of the United States and is the basic source of data for revising the items and weights in the market basket of consumer purchases to be priced for the Consumer Price Index. CES data provide detailed data on expenditures and income of consumers, as well as the demographic characteristics of those consumers. The survey does not provide state estimates, but it does provide regional estimates. Thus, the estimates are broken down into four regions—Northeast, Midwest, South, and West—to account for the differences in the cost of living across various parts of the country.[12] Consequently, an expense value is calculated using actual experience of the elderly for each region, family size, and income level by averaging the observed expenses for the elderly within each category meeting the above criteria. The housing expenses are further broken down by whether the elderly own or rent their home. The basic health expenditure category has additional data needs beyond the CES.[13]

The total deterministic expenses for elderly individual or family are then the sum of the value in all the expense categories for family size, family income level, and region of the individual or family. These expenses make up the basic annual (recurring) expenses for the individual or family. However, if the individual or family meet the income and asset tests for Medicaid, Medicaid is assumed to cover the basic health care expenses (both parts), not those of the individual or family. Furthermore, Part B premium relief for the low-income elderly (not qualifying for Medicaid) is also incorporated.

Stochastic Retirement Expenditures

The second component of health expenditures is the result of simulated health events that would require long-term care in a nursing home or home-based setting for the elderly. Neither of these simulated types of care would be reimbursed by Medicare because they would be for custodial (not rehabilitative) care.

For determining whether an individual has these expenses, the following process is undertaken. An individual reaching the Social Security normal retirement age has a probability of being in one of four possible assumed "health" conditions, based on the estimates of the use of each type of care from the surveys above and mortality:

- Not receiving either home health or nursing home care.
- Home health care patient.
- Nursing home care patient.
- Death.

The individual is randomly assigned to each of these four categories with the likelihood of falling into one of the four categories based upon the estimated probabilities of each event. If the individual does not need long-term care, no stochastic expenses are incurred. Each year, the individual will again face these probabilities (the probabilities of being in the different conditions will change as the individual becomes older after reaching age 75 then again at age 85). This continues until death or the need for long-term care.

For those who have a resulting status of home health care or nursing home care, the duration of care is simulated. After the duration of care for a nursing home stay or episode of home health care, the individual will have a probability of being discharged to one of the other three conditions. The stochastic expenses incurred are then determined by the length of the stay/number of days of care times the per diem charge estimated for the nursing home care and home health care, respectively, in each region.

For any person without the need for long-term care, this process repeats annually. The process repeats for individuals receiving home health care or nursing home care at the end of their duration of stay/care and subsequently if not receiving the specialized care again at their next birthday. Those who are simulated to die, of course, are not further simulated.

As with the basic health care expenses, the qualification of Medicaid by income and asset levels is considered to see how much of the stochastic expenses must be covered by the individual to determine the individual's final expenditures for the care. Only those expenditures attributable to the individual□not the Medicaid program□are considered as expenses to the individual and as a result are included any of the "deficit" calculations.

Total Retirement Expenses

The elderly individual or families' expenses are then the sum of their assumed deterministic expenses based upon their demographic characteristics plus any simulated stochastic expenses that they may have incurred. In each subsequent year of life, the total expenditures are again calculated in this manner. The base year's expenditure value estimates excluding the health care expenses are adjusted annually using the assumed general inflation rate of 3.3 percent from the 2001 OASDI Trustees Report, while the health care expenses are adjusted annually using the 4.0 percent medical consumer price index that corresponds to the June 2002–June 2003 level.[14,15]

Comparison of Retirement Income and Retirement Expenses

The primary objective of this analysis is to combine the simulated retirement *income and wealth* with the simulated retiree *expenditures* to determine how much each family unit would need to save today (as percentage of their current wages) to maintain a prespecified "comfort level" (i.e., confidence level) that they will be able to able to afford the simulated expenses for the remainder of the lifetime of the family unit (i.e., death of second spouse in a family). These savings rates are reported by age cohort and gender. Six five-year birth cohorts are simulated. The oldest group was born in the period 1936 to 1940 inclusive (currently ages 66 to 70), while the youngest group was born in the period 1961 to 1965 (currently ages 41 to 45), inclusive. In addition, the relative income was reported by estimating lifetime income quartiles (from 2002 though retirement age) for each of the combinations of birth cohort and gender.

It is important to note that within each of the groups modeled there will undoubtedly be significant percentages in the zero category, as well as those at levels far higher than most individuals could possibly save. These situations are accounted for in two ways: First, medians are reported for each of the groups; in other words, the numbers presented in Figures 8 and 9 provide a number representing the estimate for the 75th or 90th percentile when ranked by percentage of compensation. Second, the reported values are limited to 25 percent of compensation under the assumption that few, if any, family units would be able to contribute in excess of this percentage on a continuous basis until retirement age.

It is also important to note that these percentages merely represent savings that need to be generated *in addition to* what retirement income and/or wealth is simulated by the model. Therefore, if the family unit is already generating savings for retirement *beyond what is included* in defined benefit or defined contribution plans, IRAs, Social Security and/or net housing equity, that value needs to be deducted from the estimated percentages.

After the retirement income and wealth was simulated for each family unit, 1,000 observations were simulated (from retirement age until death of the individual for single males and single females or the second person to die for families), and the present value of the aggregated deficits at retirement age were computed. At that point, the observations were rank-ordered in terms of the present value of the deficits, and the 75th and 90th percentiles of the distribution were determined. Next, the future simulated retirement income accumulated to retirement age was determined, and the information used to determine the percentage of compensation that would need to be saved to have sufficient additional income to offset the present value of accumulated deficits for the 75th and 90th percentiles of the distribution.

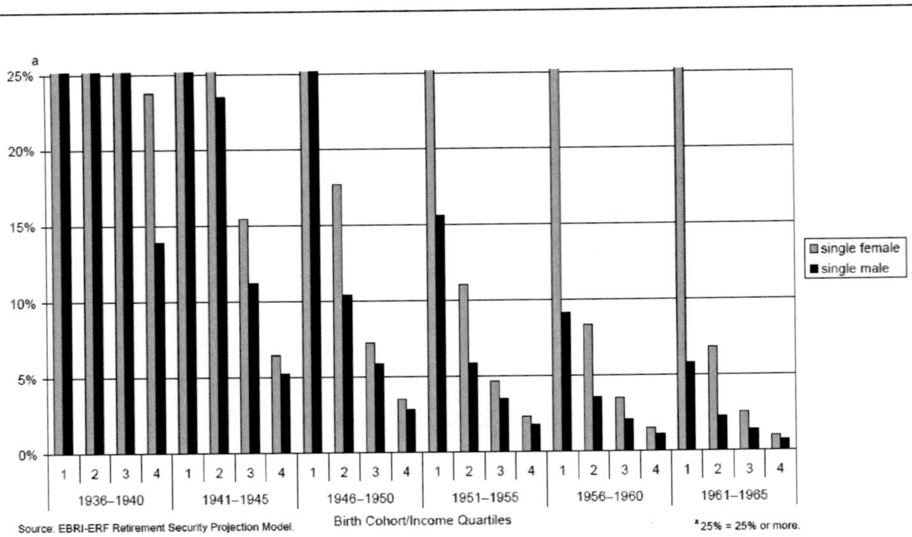

Figure 8. Percentage of Added Compensation That Must Be Saved Annually Until Retirement For a 75% Chance of Covering Basic Retirement Expenses (assumes current Social Security and housing equity is never liquidated).

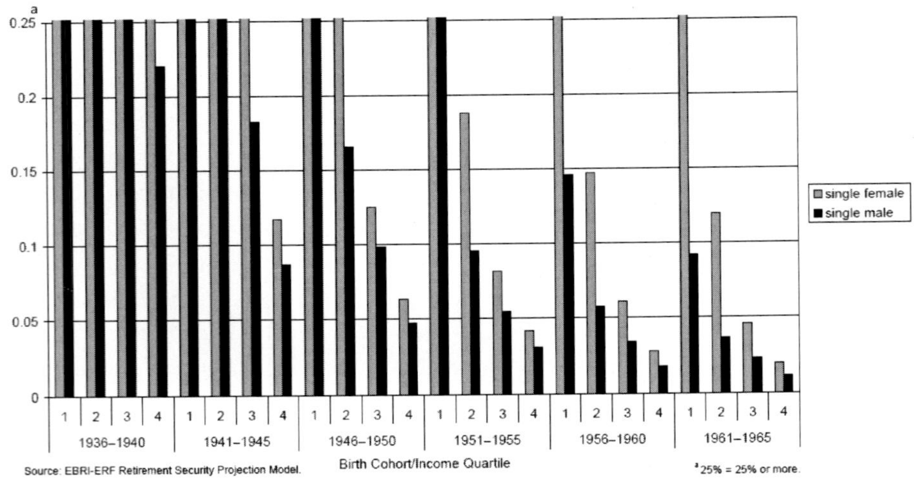

Figure 9. Percentage of Added Compensation That Must Be Saved Annually Until Retirement For a 90% Chance of Covering Basic Retirement Expenses (assumes current Social Security and housing equity is never liquidated).

RESULTS

Figure 8 shows the median percentage of compensation that must be saved each year until retirement for a 75 percent chance that there will be adequate retirement income when combined with simulated retirement wealth, assuming current Social Security benefits and that housing equity is never liquidated. For example, both genders in the first two income quartiles for the oldest birth cohort are at the 25 percent of compensation threshold. For those in the highest income quartile for this birth cohort, the percentages of additional annual compensation needed to be saved are 23.8 percent for single females and 13.9 percent for single males.

Figure 9 shows the additional savings required to provide retirement adequacy in 9 out of 10 simulated life paths. In this case, all the medians for both genders in the first three income quartiles are at the threshold. Those in the highest income quartile for this birth cohort all have requirements that would prove difficult if not impossible to implement: Single females are estimated to now need to save more than 25 percent of compensation and single males 22.1 percent of compensation. Given that most individuals would be unlikely to choose a situation that would provide them with adequate retirement income only 50 percent of the time, this analysis focuses only on the 75 percent and 90 percent confidence levels.[16]

REFERENCES

[1] Jack L. VanDerhei and Craig Copeland, , "Can America Afford Tomorrow's Retirees: Results From the EBRI-ERF Retirement Security Projection Model," *EBRI Issue Brief* no.263, November 2003.

[2] http://socialsecurity.gov/pressoffice/factsheets/women.htm, last accessed 3/9/2006.

[3] Social Security provides both survivorship and disability benefits in addition to retirement benefits. See www.ssa.gov for additional details.

[4] SSA states that the median earnings of full-time women workers in 2002 was $30,203 compared with $39,429 for men; however, they also note that this disparity has closed substantially in the past four decades during which period today's retirees would have generated their working histories necessary to calculate Social Security benefits.

[5] Private pensions include survivor, disability, and retirement income pensions from corporate or union sponsors. In addition, *regular* payments from individual retirement accounts (IRAs), Keoghs, and 401(k)-type accounts are included in private pensions. Public pensions include payments from survivor, disability, and retirement income pensions from federal, U.S. military, and state or local sponsors. Other pension income includes survivor payments from U.S. railroad retirement, workers' compensation, Black Lung, regular payments from estates, trusts, annuities, or life insurance, and other survivor payments; disability payments from U.S. railroad retirement, accidental or disability insurance, Black Lung, workers' compensation, state temporary sickness, and other disability payments; and retirement payments from U.S. railroad, regular payments from annuities or paid-up insurance policies, and other retirement payments. These three sources of pension income are combined to determine the percentage of those 65 or older with pension income.

[6] This analysis is based on the U.S. Census Bureau's March 2005 Current Population Survey (CPS) and appeared in Craig Copeland, "Employment-Based Retirement Plan Participation: Geographic Differences and Trends, 2004," *EBRI Issue Brief* ,(October 2005).

[7] Craig Copeland, "Retirement Plan Participation and Retirees' Perception of Their Standard of Living, *EBRI Issue Brief*, January 2006.

[8] Sheila Campbell and Alicia H. Munnell, “Sex and 401(K) Plans,” *Just The Facts On Retirement Issues* (No. 4, May 2002), Center for Retirement Research at Boston College.

[9] See Jack L. VanDerhei, "Measuring Retirement Income Adequacy, Part One: Traditional Replacement Ratios and Results for Workers at Large Companies," *EBRI Notes* no. 9, September 2004.

[10] Replacement ratios typically attempt to provide an indication of the percentage of income earned just prior to retirement that will be replaced in retirement. This typically involves a numerator that combines annuity payments from Social Security and defined benefit plans with an annuitized amount from defined contribution and IRAs. The denominator will be based on an average of final earnings just prior to retirement age.

[11] Unlike many other models, the model used in this analysis does NOT merely assume that a retiree will survive to his or her average life expectancy. Unfortunately, results generated under these assumptions would provide the amount necessary to pay for retirement expenditures only approximately 50 percent of the time. Instead, this model considers the entire distribution of possible future lifetimes on a gender-specific basis and allows the concept of longevity risk to be explicitly modeled.

[12] The Northeast region includes the states of Maine, New Hampshire, Vermont, Massachusetts, Rhode Island, Connecticut, New York, New Jersey, and Pennsylvania. The Midwest region includes the states of Ohio, Indiana, Illinois, Michigan, Wisconsin, Minnesota, Iowa, Missouri, North Dakota, South Dakota, Nebraska, and Kansas. The South region includes the states of Delaware, Maryland, District of Columbia, Virginia, West Virginia, North Carolina, South Carolina, Georgia, Florida, Kentucky, Tennessee, Alabama, Mississippi, Arkansas, Louisiana, Oklahoma, and Texas; while the West region includes the states of Montana, Idaho, Wyoming, Colorado, New Mexico, Arizona, Utah, Nevada, Washington, Oregon, California, Alaska, and Hawaii.

[13] For more detail see Jack L. VanDerhei and Craig Copeland, “Can America Afford Tomorrow's Retirees: Results From the EBRI-ERF Retirement Security Projection Model,” *EBRI Issue Brief* no.263, November 2003.

[14] The 2003 OASDI Trustees report subsequently reduced the assumed general inflation rate to 3.0 percent. The actuaries at the Center for Medicare & Medicaid Services developed a personal health care chain-type index that is a composite index of health care prices in the overall health care economy, which they predict will rise at a 3.5 percent level annually from 2004–2008 and 3.9 percent annually from 2009–20 12.

[15] While the medical consumer price index only accounts for the increases in prices of the health care services, it does not account for the changes in the number and/or intensity of services obtained. Thus, with increased longevity, the rate of health care expenditure growth will be significantly higher than the 4.0 percent medical inflation rate, as has been the case in recent years.

[16] For additional detail on how these findings differ by assumptions for the use of housing equity to pay retirement expenses as well as alternative approaches to Social Security reform, see Jack L. VanDerhei and Craig Copeland, “Can America Afford Tomorrow's Retirees: Results From the EBRI-ERF Retirement Security Projection Model,” *EBRI Issue Brief* no.263, November 2003.

In: Challenges Women Face in Retirement Security
Editor: Jean B. Larou, pp. 49-60
ISBN: 978-1-60741-747-7

Chapter 9

WHAT EVERY WOMAN SHOULD KNOW*

Social Security Administration

WHAT SOCIAL SECURITY MEANS TO YOU

Social Security plays an important role in providing economic security for women. Nearly 60 percent of the people receiving Social Security benefits are women. In the 21st century, more women work, pay Social Security taxes and earn credit toward monthly retirement income than at any other time in our nation's history.

Today, women have challenging choices to make. Some may spend their entire adulthood in a career or job outside the home. Some may work for a few years, leave the labor force to raise children and eventually return to work. And some may choose not to work outside of the home. Whether they work, have worked or have never worked, it is essential that women understand how Social Security can help them and their families.

Women tend to care for many people—spouses, children and parents. And although they have made significant strides, women are more likely to earn less over their lifetimes than men. They are less often covered by private retirement plans and more dependent on Social Security—and for a longer period of time since, on average, women live about five years longer than men.

Social Security offers a basic level of protection to all women covered by this program. When women work, they pay taxes into the Social Security system, providing for their own benefits. In addition, their husbands' earnings can give them Social Security coverage as well. Women who do not work are often covered through their husbands' work and can receive benefits when they retire, become disabled or die.

Over the years, the level of Social Security protection for women has been strengthened. For example, the amount of benefits for a surviving spouse was raised and benefits for disabled spouses also increased. Economic protection for divorced women improved with the removal of the requirement that the divorced wife must be dependent on her husband. Also,

---

* This is an edited, reformatted and augmented version of Social Security Administration Publication No. 05-10127 dated January 2009.

the number of years the couple must be married in order for the divorced spouse to qualify for benefits decreased.

Besides understanding the benefits to which they may be entitled, women also need to be aware of other aspects of the Social Security program. They need to know about providing Social Security coverage for anyone they may hire as a household worker or childcare provider. And they need to know some basics like what to do if they change their names.

While Social Security is a vital program, especially for women, it was never intended to cover all of their financial needs. To live comfortably, everyone needs to plan accordingly. Living within one's means and saving for the future are big parts of that plan.

Your Social Security Record and Number

Each year your employer sends a copy of your W-2 (Wage and Tax Statement) to Social Security. We compare your name and Social Security number on the W-2 with the information in our files. We add the earnings shown on the W-2 to your Social Security record.

It is critical that your name and Social Security number on your Social Security card agree with your employer's payroll records and W-2 so that we can credit your earnings to your record. It is up to you to make sure that both Social Security's records and your employer's records are correct. If your Social Security card is incorrect, contact any Social Security office to make changes. Check your W-2 form to make sure your employer's record is correct and, if it is not, give your employer the accurate information.

If you are a worker age 25 or older and not receiving benefits, you receive a *Social Security Statement* every year that can be a valuable tool to help you plan a secure financial future. It provides you with a record of your earnings and gives estimates of what your Social Security benefits would be at different retirement ages.

It also gives an estimate of the disability benefits you could receive if you become severely disabled before retirement, as well as estimates of the survivors benefits Social Security would provide your spouse and eligible family members when you die. Review this *Statement* to make sure that all of your earnings are included. If your *Statement* does not include all of your earnings, let your employer and your Social Security office know about any incorrect information.

If You Change Your Name

Whenever you change your name, be sure to report the change to Social Security. Otherwise, your earnings may not be recorded properly and you may not receive all the Social Security you are due. Not changing your name with Social Security also can delay your income tax refund.

To report a name change, fill out an *Application for a Social Security Card* (Form SS-5). You can get the form by visiting ***www.socialsecurity.gov*** on the Internet or any Social Security office or by calling Social Security's toll-free number, **1-800-772-1213**.

You must show us a recently issued document as proof of your legal name change. Documents Social Security may accept to prove a legal name change include:

- Marriage document;
- Divorce decree;
- Certificate of Naturalization showing a new name; or
- Court order for a name change.

If the document you provide for a legal name change does not give enough information to identify you or if you legally changed your name more than two years ago, then you also must show us two identity documents including:

- One document in your old name; and
- A second document with your new legal name.

In addition to your name, these documents also must contain identifying information or a recent photograph.

If you are a U.S. citizen born outside the United States and our records do not show you are a citizen, you will need to provide proof of your U.S. citizenship. If you are not a U.S. citizen, Social Security will ask to see your current immigration documents.

The new card will have the same number as your previous card, but will show your new name.

If You Are a Victim of Family Violence

People in all walks of life can be victims of family violence or harassment, abuse or life-endangering situations. If you are a victim of family violence, Social Security may be able to help you.

Public awareness campaigns stress how important it is for victims to develop safety plans that include gathering personal papers and choosing a safe place to go. Sometimes the best way to evade an abuser and reduce the risk of further violence may be to relocate and establish a new identity. Following these changes, it also may be helpful to get a new Social Security number.

Although Social Security does not routinely assign new numbers, we will do so when evidence shows you are being harassed or abused or your life is endangered.

Applying for a new number is a big decision. It may impact your ability to interact with federal and state agencies, employers and others. This is because your financial, medical, employment and other records will be under your former Social Security number and name (if you change your name). If you expect to change your name, we recommend you do so before applying for a new number.

For more information, ask for *New Numbers For Domestic Violence Victims* (Publication No. 05-10093).

Social Security Numbers for Children

It is a good idea to apply for a Social Security number for your baby when you apply for your baby's birth certificate. Social Security will mail the card to you. Or, you can wait and apply at any Social Security office. If you wait, you must provide evidence of your child's age, identity and U.S. citizenship status, as well as proof of your identity. We must verify your child's birth record, which can add up to 12 weeks to the time it takes to issue a card. To verify a birth record, Social Security will contact the office that issued it.

What Your Social Security Taxes Pay for

When you work and pay Social Security taxes, you earn Social Security credits that can count toward your retirement benefits and can qualify you and your family for disability and survivors insurance coverage. In addition, when you pay Medicare taxes, you are earning Medicare protection that can be available to you when you reach age 65 or if you become disabled. Social Security's benefit package includes:

- Retirement benefits that are paid each month to retired workers as early as age 62.
- Disability benefits that are paid each month to workers of all ages who have a severe disability.
- In some cases, a young worker may qualify for a disability benefit with as little as one and one-half years of work.
- Family benefits that are paid each month to the spouse and children of retired or disabled workers.
- Survivors benefits that are paid each month to the widow or widower and children of a deceased worker. In some cases, the family of a young deceased worker can receive these benefits even if the worker had as few as one and one-half years of work.
- Medicare, which helps with hospital bills and provides limited coverage for skilled nursing facility stays and hospice care. It also can cover doctors' services and prescription drugs.

Some Special Employment Situations

Self-Employed

Most people who pay into Social Security work for an employer. Their employer deducts Social Security taxes from their paycheck, matches that contribution and sends taxes to the Internal Revenue Service (IRS) and reports wages to Social Security. But self-employed people must report their earnings and pay their taxes directly to IRS.

You are self-employed if you operate a trade, business or profession, either by yourself or as a partner. You report your earnings for Social Security when you file your federal income tax return. If your net earnings are $400 or more in a year, you must report your earnings on Schedule SE, in addition to the other tax forms you must file.

If you and your husband operate a business together, you are entitled to receive Social Security credits as a partner. Be sure to file a separate Schedule SE, even though you and your husband file a joint income tax return. If you do not file a separate self-employment report, you will not get Social Security benefits from your own work, because all of the earnings will be reported on your husband's record.

Household Workers

Some household workers are covered under Social Security depending on how much they earn. Household workers include babysitters, maids, cooks, laundry workers, butlers, gardeners, chauffeurs and people who do housecleaning or repair work. Household workers who are under age 18 during any part of the year and who do not do household work as a principal job are not covered under Social Security.

If you hire household workers, make sure you accurately record their Social Security numbers, withhold Social Security taxes from their wages, pay an equal amount and send the combined taxes to IRS using your own federal income tax return.

If you are a household worker, make sure your employer is paying Social Security taxes for you. You should receive a form W-2 from your employer by January 31 of the year following the year you did the work. For more information, ask for *Household Workers* (Publication No. 05-10021).

Military Service

If you have served in the military on active duty or on inactive duty for training since 1957, you paid into Social Security. Inactive duty service in the Armed Forces Reserves and National Guard weekend drills have been covered by Social Security since 1988. If you served in the military before 1957, you did not pay into Social Security directly, but your records may be credited with special earnings for Social Security purposes that count toward any benefits you may receive.

When you apply for Social Security, the credits you receive for military service are added to your civilian work credits. The number of credits you have determines whether you qualify for Social Security.

You may be eligible for both Social Security benefits and military retirement. Generally, there is no reduction of Social Security benefits because of your military retirement. You will get your full Social Security benefits based on your earnings.

Social Security survivors benefits may affect benefits payable under the optional Department of Defense Survivors Benefit Plan. You should check with the Department of Defense or your military retirement advisor for more information.

When You Retire

Most people need 10 years of work (40 credits) to qualify for benefits. Your benefit amount is based on your earnings averaged over most of your working career. Higher lifetime earnings result in higher benefits. If you have some years of no earnings or low earnings, your benefit amount may be lower than if you had worked steadily.

Your benefit also is affected by your age at the time you start receiving benefits. If you start your retirement benefits at age 62 (the earliest possible retirement age), your benefit will be lower than if you wait until your full retirement age.

If you choose to work while receiving Social Security benefits before you reach full retirement age, your benefits will be reduced by $1 for every $2 you earn over the annual limit (which increases each year). In the year you reach full retirement age, your benefits will be reduced by $1 for every $3 you earn over the limit in the months before your birthday. But once you reach full retirement age, you will get your full retirement benefits no matter how much you work and earn.

Age to receive full Social Security benefits	
Year of birth	Full retirement age
1937 or earlier	65
1938	65 and 2 months
1939	65 and 4 months
1940	65 and 6 months
1941	65 and 8 months
1942	65 and 10 months
1943-1954	66
1955	66 and 2 months
1956	66 and 4 months
1957	66 and 6 months
1958	66 and 8 months
1959	66 and 10 months
1960 or later	67

As you continue working, we will review your earnings each year and recalculate your benefit amount. Usually, your additional earnings will increase your benefit amount. If the amount increases, we will notify you and readjust your benefit payments.

If you are eligible for benefits on more than one work record, such as your own and your husband's, you generally receive the higher benefit amount. When you apply for benefits, the Social Security representative can determine which record will give you the higher benefit.

If you are eligible for a spouse's or ex-spouse's benefit and your own retirement benefit, you should file for both. (The same rule applies to your husband or ex-husband.) If your husband works past full retirement age and does not collect Social Security benefits, you can still retire and get benefits based on your own work. Then, when he does retire, you can receive bene fits on his record if they would be higher.

If your husband or ex-husband is deceased, you can choose which benefit to apply for now or choose to postpone filing for either benefit until you reach full retirement age.

If you have reached your full retirement age, and are eligible for a spouse's or ex-spouse's benefit and your own retirement benefit, you may choose to receive only spouse's benefits and continue accruing delayed retirement credits on your own Social Security record. You may then file for benefits at a later date and receive a higher monthly benefit based on the effect of delayed retirement credits. For more information on retirement, visit ***www.socialsecurity.gov/planners*** or ask for *Retirement Benefits* (Publication No. 05-10035).

You will have Medicare coverage in addition to Social Security benefits if you are eligible for benefits either on your own record or your husband's record. You will have Medicare hospital insurance (Part A) protection at age 65 and you will have the opportunity to buy Medicare medical insurance (Part B) for a monthly premium. You can also enroll in a Medicare Advantage Plan (Part C) and a Medicare prescription drug plan (Part D). If you are not eligible for benefits and you do not have enough credits, you can pay a monthly premium to buy Medicare coverage. For more information, ask for *Medicare* (Publication No. 05-10043).

If You Become Disabled

If you become disabled, you may be able to get disability benefits if you have worked long enough and recently enough under Social Security. The amount of work you need increases with age. You need credit for one and one-half years of work out of the past three years if you become disabled before age 24 and up to five out of the last 10 years if you become disabled at age 31 or older. Some women lose their disability coverage when they move in and out of the workforce and do not meet the recent work requirement. If you need help figuring out how much work you need to maintain your disability coverage, call your local Social Security office.

You will be considered disabled if you cannot do work that you did before and we decide that you cannot adjust to other work because of your medical condition(s). Your disability also must last, or be expected to last, for at least a year or to result in death. After you receive disability payments for 24 consecutive months, you also will have Medicare protection.

Military service members can receive expedited processing of disability claims from Social Security. Benefits available through Social Security are different than those from the Department of Veterans Affairs and require a separate application. The expedited process is used for military service members who became disabled while on active military service on or after October 1, 2001, regardless of where the disability occurs.

For more information on disability programs, visit ***www.socialsecurity.gov/disability*** or ask for *Disability Benefits* (Publication No. 05-10029). For more information on disability benefits for wounded warriors, visit ***www.socialsecurity.gov/ woundedwarriors*** or ask for *Disability Benefits For Wounded Warriors* (Publication No. 05-10030).

When You Are Ready to Apply

Online Services

You can apply for Social Security retirement, disability or spouse's benefits, or any combination of those benefits online. You will complete and sign the application electronically. We will let you know which benefits you are entitled to after we receive your application.

Direct Deposit

Social Security benefits are generally paid by direct deposit. Direct deposit is a simple, safe and secure way to receive your benefits. Be sure to have your checkbook or account statement with you when you apply. We will need that information to make sure your monthly benefit is correctly deposited into your account.

Benefits for Your Family

When you start receiving Social Security retirement or disability benefits, other family members also may be eligible for payments. For example, benefits can be paid to your husband:

- If he is age 62 or older; or
- At any age if he is caring for your child (the child must be younger than age 16 or disabled and receiving Social Security benefits on your record).

Benefits also can be paid to your unmarried children if they are:

- Younger than age 18;
- Between age 18 and age 19, but in elementary or secondary school as full-time students; or
- Age 18 or older and severely disabled (the disability must have started before age 22).

If You Should Die

If you should die, your family may be eligible for benefits based on your work. Family members who can collect benefits include a widower who is:

- Age 60 or older; or
- Age 50 or older and disabled; or
- Any age if he is caring for your child who is younger than age 16 or disabled and receiving Social Security benefits.

Your children can receive benefits, too, if they are unmarried and:

- Younger than age 18; or

- Between age 18 and age 19, but in an elementary or secondary school as full-time students; or
- Age 18 or older and severely disabled (the disability must have started before age 22).

Additionally, your parents can receive benefits on your earnings if they were dependent on you for at least half of their support.

If you had enough credits, a one-time payment of $255 also will be made after your death. This benefit may be paid to your spouse or minor children if they meet certain requirements.

For more information, ask for *Survivors Benefits* (Publication No. 05-10084).

If You Have Income from a Government Pension

If you worked at a job where you did not pay Social Security taxes, two laws may affect your Social Security benefits.

- The Windfall Elimination Provision affects the way your Social Security retirement or disability benefits are figured. It applies to you only if you receive Social Security benefits based on your own earnings and you are receiving the other pension.
- Government Pension Offset affects only the Social Security benefits you could receive based on your husband's earnings.

For more information about the Windfall Elimination Provision, the Government Pension Offset and WEP and GPO online calculators visit ***www.socialsecurity.gov/gpo-wep***. Benefit calculators are also available at ***www.socialsecurity.gov/planners/ calculators.htm***. You also can ask for *Windfall Elimination Provision* (Publication No. 05-10045) and *Government Pension Offset* (Publication No. 05-10007).

If You Have Not Worked or Do Not Have Enough Social Security Credits

If you have not worked or do not have enough Social Security credits and you are married, you may be eligible for Social Security benefits as a result of your husband's work. You and your children (younger than age 18 or younger than age 19 if still in secondary school or disabled before age 22) have Social Security protection through your husband's work. When he retires, or if he becomes disabled, you could be eligible for benefits as early as age 62. If you are caring for your child who is younger than age 16 or disabled and entitled to benefits, you could receive benefits at any age.

If you choose to begin receiving wife's benefits before you reach full retirement age, your benefit amount will be reduced and will not be increased once you reach full retirement age. If you wait until you reach full retirement age, you will receive the maximum benefit, which is up to half of the amount your husband is entitled to receive at his full retirement age.

You and your husband will be eligible for Medicare at age 65. ***NOTE:*** *If your husband is full retirement age, he can apply for retirement benefits and then request to have payments suspended. That way, you can receive a spouse's benefits and he can continue to earn delayed retirement credits until age 70.*

If You Become a Widow

If your husband dies, you can get widow's benefits if you are age 60 or older. If you are disabled, you can get widow's benefits as early as age 50. Your benefit amount will depend on your age and on the amount your deceased husband was entitled to when he died. If he was receiving reduced benefits, your survivor benefit will be based on that amount.

If you are a widow with children, you may be eligible for a widow's benefit at any age when you are caring for a child who is younger than 16 or disabled and entitled to benefits. As a widow, you also may be eligible for Medicare at age 65. If you remarry before you reach age 60 (or age 50 if disabled), you cannot receive widow's benefits as long as that marriage remains in effect.

If you remarry after you reach age 60 (or age 50 if disabled), you will continue to receive benefits on your deceased husband's Social Security record. However, if your current husband is a Social Security beneficiary, you should apply for a wife's benefit on his record if it would be larger than your widow's benefit. You cannot get both.

If you are also entitled to retirement benefits based on your own work, you have some other options. Ask a Social Security representative to explain the options, so you can decide which would be best for you.

If You Are Divorced

If you have never asked Social Security about receiving benefits based on your ex-husband's work, you should do so. Many women get a higher benefit based on their ex-husband's work, especially if he is deceased. When you apply, you will need to give his Social Security number. If you do not know his number, you will need to provide his date and place of birth and his parents' names.

The following requirements also apply to your divorced husband if his eligibility for benefits is based on your work.

If Your Ex-Husband Is Living–

If you are divorced, you can receive benefits based on your ex-husband's work if—

- Your marriage lasted 10 years or longer;
- You are unmarried;
- You are age 62 or older;

- The benefit you are entitled to receive based on your own work is less than the benefits you would receive on your husband's work; and
- Your ex-husband is entitled to Social Security retirement or disability benefits.

If he has not applied for benefits, but can qualify for them and is age 62 or older, you can receive benefits on his work if you have been divorced from him for at least two years.

If Your Ex-Husband Is Deceased, You Can Receive Benefits–

- At age 60, or age 50 if you are disabled, if your marriage lasted at least 10 years, and you are not entitled to a higher benefit on your own record.
- At any age if you are caring for his child who also is your natural or legally adopted child and younger than 16 or disabled and entitled to benefits. Your benefits will continue until the child reaches age 16 or is no longer disabled. You can receive this benefit even though you were not married to your ex-husband for 10 years.

If You Have Limited Income

If you are age 65 or older, or blind or disabled, and your income and the value of your resources is limited, you may be eligible to receive monthly payments under the Supplemental Security Income (SSI) program. Generally, to receive SSI you must be living in the United States or the Northern Mariana Islands and be a U.S. citizen. Certain noncitizens also may be eligible to receive SSI. To learn more about SSI, ask for *Supplemental Security Income* (Publication No. 05-11000).

If you have a limited income and few resources, your state can decide whether you qualify for help with Medicare expenses under the Medicare Savings Programs. If you think you may qualify, contact your state or local medical assistance (Medicaid) agency, social services program or welfare office. Also, more information is available from the Centers for Medicare & Medicaid Services (CMS). Ask for *If you need help paying Medicare costs, there are programs that can help you save money* (Publication No. CMS 10126) by calling the Medicare toll-free number, **1-800-MEDICARE (1-800-633-4227)**. If you are deaf or hard of hearing, you may call TTY **1-877-486-2048**.

You also may be able to get extra help paying for the Medicare prescription drug program. Anyone who has Medicare can get Medicare prescription drug coverage. Extra help is available for some people with limited income and resources and will pay for all or most of the monthly premiums, annual deductibles and prescription co-payments related to their plan. Many people with limited income and resources qualify for these big savings and do not even know it. To find out if you are eligible, Social Security will need to know your income and the value of your savings, investments and real estate (other than your home). If you are married and living with your spouse, we will need this information for both of you.

Even if you do not qualify for the extra help, you may be able to help someone you care about apply for extra help with their Medicare prescription drug costs.

For more information, ask for *Getting Help With Medicare Prescription Drug Plan Costs, Income And Resource Limits* (Publication No. 05-10115).

If You Are a Caregiver

If you are caring for an elderly or disabled relative who needs help managing their monthly Social Security or SSI benefits, you can apply to be representative payee. Social Security will conduct a careful investigation to determine if you meet the requirements.

As a representative payee, we will pay you the person's benefits to use on his or her behalf. Therefore, you must know what your relative's needs are so you can decide how benefits can best be used for his or her personal care and well-being. First, you must make sure that food and shelter are provided. Then, you can use the money to pay medical and dental bills not covered by health insurance and for personal needs and recreation.

For more information about the representative payee program, visit ***www.socialsecurity.gov/payee***. You also can ask for *A Guide For Representative Payees* (Publication No. 05-10076). If you are caring for a child with disabilities, ask for *Benefits For Children With Disabilities* (Publication No. 05-10026).

Protection of Personal Information

Social Security keeps personal and confidential information—names, Social Security numbers, earnings records, ages and beneficiary addresses—for millions of people. Generally, we will discuss your information only with you. When you call or visit us, we will ask you several questions to help us verify your identity. If you want someone else to help with your Social Security business, we need your permission to discuss your information with that person. You should treat your Social Security number as confidential information and avoid giving it out unnecessarily.

You should keep your Social Security card in a safe place with your other important papers. Do not carry it with you unless you need to show it to an employer or service provider.

More Information

For more information specifically geared toward women, visit ***www.socialsecurity.gov/women***.

In: Challenges Women Face in Retirement Security
Editor: Jean B. Larou, pp. 61-65
ISBN: 978-1-60741-747-7

Chapter 10

WOMEN AND RETIREMENT SAVINGS*

U.S. Department of Labor

Planning and saving for retirement may seem like goals that are far in the future. Yet saving, especially for retirement, should start early and continue throughout your lifetime. Here are four reasons why saving matters to women—and especially to you!

DO YOU KNOW?

- Women are more likely to work in part-time jobs that don't qualify for a retirement plan. And working women are more likely than men to interrupt their careers to take care of family members. Therefore, they work fewer years and contribute less toward their retirement, resulting in lower lifetime savings. If you work and if you qualify, join a retirement plan now.
- Of the 62 million wage and salaried women (age 21 to 64) working in the United States, just 45 percent participated in a retirement plan. Remember, even small amounts can earn interest and add up over time.
- On average, a female at age 65 can expect to live another 19 years, 3 years longer than a man the same age. Savings can increase a woman's chances of having enough money to last during her retirement.
- By and large, women invest more conservatively than men. Choose carefully where you put your money and learn how to improve your investment returns.

START HERE...START NOW

Here are eight questions to help you think about retirement and take charge of your financial future:

* This is an edited, reformatted and augmented version a U.S. Department of Labor publication dated October 2008.

Do You Work for an Employer that Offers a Retirement Plan?

If your employer offers a retirement plan, join it as soon as you can and contribute as much as the plan allows. Most employers with a 401(k) plan match a fixed percentage of the employee's contribution. The most common match is 50 percent of the employee's contribution up to a maximum percentage of wages or salary (usually 6 percent). The majority of employers offer 50 percent or more. That's like getting free money! While all job categories may not be included in your employer's plan (those of part-time or temporary workers, for instance), your job may be one that is.

Remember, by saving early, you have time on your side. Your savings will grow and your earnings will compound over time.

Have You Worked at the Job Long Enough to Earn Retirement Benefits?

In many companies, you may have to work for 5 years to become eligible to receive retirement benefits. Some workplaces have a shorter vesting period (vesting simply means that you have worked long enough to earn the right to benefits from a savings or pension plan).

Too often employees, especially women, quit work, transfer to another job, or interrupt their work lives just short of the time required to become vested. Ask the personnel office, retirement plan administrator, or union representative about the vesting period and other details of your company's plan.

Do You Keep Copies of the Documents that Define the Provisions of Your Retirement Plan?

In addition to asking questions of company or retirement plan officials, you should keep copies of the summary plan description (SPD) and any amendments. The SPD is a document that retirement plan administrators are required to prepare, and it outlines your benefits and how they are calculated. The SPD also spells out the financial consequences - usually a reduction in benefits - if you decide to retire early (earlier than age 65 in many plans). You probably received a copy of the SPD when you joined the pension or savings plan, but you may request another one from your employer or plan administrator. Also remember to keep retirementrelated records from all jobs. They provide valuable information about your benefit rights, even when you no longer work for a company.

What Happens to Your Retirement Benefits if You Change Jobs?

You may lose the retirement benefits you have earned if you leave your job before you are vested. However, once vested, you have the right to receive benefits even when you leave your job. In such cases, the company may allow, or in certain cases may insist, that you take your retirement benefits in a lump sum when you leave. However, other companies may not permit you to receive your money until retirement. The rules for your plan are spelled out in the SPD.

A word of caution: If you receive your retirement benefits in a lump sum, you will owe additional income taxes, and may owe a penalty tax. A better way is to reinvest your savings in another qualified retirement plan or an Individual Retirement Account (IRA) within 60 days. You avoid tax penalties and you keep your long-term retirement goals on track.

If you do want to reinvest the money, it is important that you do not directly receive it. If you receive the money directly, you will have to pay a 20 percent withholding tax on the amount you receive and then file for a refund in the next year, providing proof that you have transferred the funds to an IRA. Instead, instruct the retirement plan to transfer your money directly to an IRA you have established or to another qualified retirement plan. This is easy to do using simple forms supplied by the new plan. If you want help with the forms, representatives of the plan are generally available to assist you.

Do You Know How You Can Save for Retirement even if You Don't Belong to an Employer-Sponsored Retirement Plan?

Anyone receiving compensation or married to someone receiving compensation can contribute to an IRA. In addition, if you are self-employed, you can start a Simplified Employment Plan (SEP), or a Savings Incentive Match Plan for Employees of Small Employers (SIMPLE).

As with other retirement savings plans, there may be tax consequences, and possibly penalties, if you withdraw your savings early.

Are You Tracking Your Social Security Earnings?

More women than ever work, pay Social Security taxes, and earn credit toward a monthly income at retirement. These earnings can mean some income for you and your family in the form of monthly benefits if you become disabled and can no longer work. If you die, your survivors may be eligible for benefits. In addition, you may be eligible for Social Security benefits through your husband's work and can receive benefits when he retires or if he becomes disabled or dies. Special rules apply if you and your husband have been employed and both have paid into Social Security. Special rules also apply if you are divorced or if you have a government retirement plan.

To calculate your benefit estimate, visit the Social Security Administration's Web site at www.socialsecurity.gov.

Are You Entitled to a Portion of Your Spouse's Retirement Benefit if You and Your Husband Divorce?

As part of a divorce or legal separation, you may be able to obtain rights to a portion of your spouse's retirement benefit (or he may be able to obtain a portion of yours). In most private-sector plans, this is done using a qualified domestic relations order (QDRO) issued by the court. You or your attorney should consult your spouse's plan administrator to determine what requirements the QDRO must meet.

Are You Aware of the Rules that Govern Your Retirement Plan and the Retirement Plan of Your Spouse if Either of You Dies?

The rules are different for defined contribution and defined benefit plans.

If you or your spouse belong to a defined benefit plan (a traditional pension plan), the surviving spouse may be entitled to receive a survivor benefit when the enrolled employee dies.

This survivor benefit is automatic unless both spouses agree, in writing, to forfeit the benefit. You will need to check the SPD or consult with the plan administrator regarding survivor annuities or other death benefits.

If you are a beneficiary under your spouse's defined benefit pension plan, you may want to request a copy of the SPD and other plan documents that describe your spouse's vested benefits. You will probably want to make the request in writing, and you may be charged a fee for the information.

The rules may be different if you or your spouse participate in a defined contribution plan (such as a 401(k) plan). Consult the plan administrator for details about spousal rights.

It's up to You

Once you've answered these questions, you're on the road to learning more about financial freedom. As a resource for women (and men), the Employee Benefits Security Administration has issued *Savings Fitness: A Guide to Your Money and Your Financial Future* and *Taking the Mystery Out of Retirement Planning*. The booklets include resource and Web site sections (see the *Resources* section to get a copy).

Resources

Employee Benefits Security Administration
U.S. Department of Labor
Publication request line: 1-866-444-EBSA (3272)
www.dol.gov/ebsa

View the following booklets on the Web site above. Request copies by calling the publication request line (above).

Top 10 Ways to Prepare for Retirement Savings Fitness: A Guide to Your Money and Your Financial Future Taking the Mystery Out of Retirement Planning What You Should Know about Your Retirement Plan Filing a Claim for Your Retirement Benefits QDROs - The Division of Retirement Benefits through Qualified Domestic Relations Orders

In addition, visit the following Web sites for more help:

Social Security Administration
Request a copy of
What Every Woman Should Know
800-772-1213
www.socialsecurity.gov

Pension Benefits Guaranty Corporation
Request a copy of
A Predictable, Secure Pension for Life
800-400-7242
www.pbgc.gov

U.S. Securities and Exchange Commission
Request a copy of
Get the Facts on Saving and Investing
800-SEC-0330
www.sec.gov

American Institute of Certified Public Accountants
360 Degrees of Financial Literacy
www.360financialliteracy.org
U.S. Financial Literacy and Education Commission
www.mymoney.gov

In: Challenges Women Face in Retirement Security
Editor: Jean B. Larou, pp. 67-130 ISBN: 978-1-60741-747-7

Chapter 11

RETIREMENT SECURITY: WOMEN FACE CHALLENGES IN ENSURING FINANCIAL SECURITY IN RETIREMENT*

United States Government Accountability Office

WHAT GAO FOUND

In general, women have less retirement income than men, largely because of women's lower labor force attachment and lower earnings, on average. Fewer women than men have income from most major retirement sources, and women have less income from these sources. Women's median Social Security income is 70 percent of men's. Also, fewer women than men have pensions. Among the population age 65 and over who continue to work, women earn just over half of what men earn. Women also have somewhat smaller income than men from assets, such as interest and dividends. Accordingly, rates of poverty among those 65 and over are substantially higher for women than for men. Although their participation has increased substantially in the last century, women still spend fewer years in the labor force than men, and they more often work part-time. Also, women tend to earn less than men, despite increases in their wages over time relative to men. Although work patterns are key in earnings differences, in prior work, we found that even after accounting for behavioral differences such as education or labor force participation, women still earn less than men.

Certain life events—including changes in marital status, labor force interruptions, and long-term care needs—can significantly reduce the amount of pension income and Social Security benefits women receive—and leave women with fewer financial resources at retirement than men. Social Security divorced spousal benefits are available only if the marriage lasted at least 10 years. Furthermore, pension benefits are available to a divorced spouse only under certain circumstances. Women's role as primary family caregiver for children and elderly relatives can reduce their career earnings, on which retirement income is

* This is an edited, reformatted and augmented version of a GAO Report GAO-08-105, dated October 2007.

based. Because women tend to live longer than men, widowhood and costly long-term care assistance may further reduce their retirement resources.

GAO's simulations of some Social Security changes that would compensate for low earnings or time out of the workforce showed that those changes tend to increase benefits for beneficiaries overall, and particularly those in lower income quintiles. Alternatively, changes that focus on shifts in family structure, such as increases in two-earner couples and increased incidence of divorce, tend to increase the benefits of groups targeted by the change, but produce mixed results for others. Some pension changes that have been proposed in the past several years take into account the changing labor force and norms of employer-provided retirement plans; while these changes are gender-neutral, they may provide important new opportunities for women to increase their retirement income. For example, decreased vesting requirements may provide additional pension income to those with intermittent workforce participation who would not qualify for pension benefits under a longer vesting schedule.

WHY GAO DID THIS STUDY

Women aged 65 and over will account for a growing segment of the U.S. population over the next several decades. Despite increases in women's workforce behavior in the past 65 years, elderly women have persistently high rates of poverty. Thus, it is important to understand the differences between men's and women's retirement income, and how women may fare given future reforms to Social Security and pensions. GAO was asked to examine (1) how women's retirement income compares with men's and the reasons for differences; (2) how certain life events such as divorce, widowhood, and workforce interruptions affect women's retirement income; and (3) the possible effect on women's retirement income of certain changes to Social Security and pensions that seek to mitigate the effects of differences in workforce participation patterns.

To address these objectives, GAO reviewed the relevant literature, interviewed academics and other retirement experts, and used a microsimulation model to project future retirement income. GAO provided a draft of this report to the departments of Labor and Treasury, the Internal Revenue Service, and the Social Security Administration. Cognizant agency officials provided technical comments which were incorporated as appropriate.

GAO is making no recommendations.

ABBREVIATIONS

AIME	Average Indexed Monthly Earnings
CSSS	Commission to Strengthen Social Security
DB	defined benefit
DC	defined contribution
ERISA	Employee Retirement Income Security Act of 1974
GEMINI	Genuine Microsimulation of Social Security and Accounts
IRA	individual retirement account
MTR	Maintain Tax Rates

OASDI	Old-Age, Survivors, and Disability Insurance
OCACT	Social Security Administration's Office of the Chief Actuary
OLC	overlapping cohorts
PENSIM	Pension Simulator
PIAP	rimary Insurance Amount
PSG	Policy Simulation Group
QDRO	qualified domestic relations order
RCS	representative cohort sample
REA	Retirement Equity Act
SPIA	Special Primary Insurance Amount
SSA	Social Security Administration
SSASIM	Social Security and Accounts Simulator
SSI	Supplemental Security Income

October 11, 2007
The Honorable Gordon Smith
Ranking Member
Senate Special Committee on Aging United States Senate

Dear Senator Smith:

Over the next 40 years women aged 65 and over will account for a growing segment of the U.S. population. In 2000, there were about 20 million women aged 65 and over, more than 7 percent of the U.S. population; by 2050 that number is estimated to grow by nearly 28 million to about 12 percent of the population. Elderly women have persistently high rates of poverty, and the major source of income for many retired women is Social Security. However, the Social Security system is affected by the decrease in the rate of growth of the working age population. Under current law, the Social Security Trustees project that by 2041 the Social Security Trust Funds could be insufficient to pay full benefits.[1]

Demographics as well as rising health care costs are profoundly affecting not only the Social Security system, but also Medicare, private pension and health benefits, and personal savings in ways that will likely present serious challenges to ensuring financial security for future retirees and, ultimately, the economic security of the nation. In recent years, many proposed reforms of the Social Security system have focused on long-term solvency and financing issues, many of which could result in decreased benefits for individuals. Alternatively, some Social Security proposals developed over the past several decades include elements that seek to modify the program and address its limitations when applied to nontraditional-family or earnings structures. These limitations may be due both to the evolving nature of families and to changes in women's labor force participation that have emerged since Social Security's creation.[2] These elements often address the needs of two-earner families as well as retirement benefits after divorce. Additionally, recent and ongoing changes in employer-sponsored pension plans, most notably the shift from defined benefit pension plans to defined contribution plans, may complement changes in workforce patterns, but also place greater responsibility for prudent savings and investment decisions on workers. Given the existing differences in men's and women's incomes, and the changes in women's workforce behavior in the later half of the 20th century, any future changes to Social Security as well as both proposed and ongoing changes to employer-provided pensions could have different impacts on women and men. It is important to understand how each will fare under various proposals.

You asked us to help clarify what drives the gap in retirement income between men and women and to provide information on the implications of different modifications to both Social Security as well as employer- provided pensions. Our objectives were to examine (1) how women's retirement income compares with men's and describe the reasons for differences; (2) how certain life events such as divorce, widowhood, and workforce interruptions affect women's retirement income, as compared with men's; and (3) the possible effect on women's retirement income of certain changes to Social Security and pensions that seek to mitigate the effects of differences in workforce participation patterns.

To address these objectives, we reviewed the relevant literature and federal laws, interviewed academics and other retirement experts, and used a retirement-income microsimulation model to project women's future retirement income.[3] Specifically, we reviewed and summarized government and academic research on women's retirement income, life events, and poverty as well as proposed changes to Social Security and employer-provided pensions. We used the Policy Simulation Group's retirement income microsimulation model to illustrate differences in benefit levels by differences in workforce attachment and marital status of a simulated population, born in 1985. We also used the microsimulation model to project changes in Social Security benefit levels for a sample of workers at age 70, from the 1950 and 1985 birth cohorts, under a variety of possible modifications. The results of our analyses reflect outcomes for individuals in the simulated populations and do not attempt to estimate outcomes for an actual population. Unlike some of our prior work, rather than evaluating Social Security reform packages that seek to achieve sustainable solvency, we evaluated proposed individual changes targeted to enhance benefits for certain groups. We also used the model to project changes in pension benefit levels for a sample of workers at age 70, from the 1985 birth cohort.[4] We used two cohorts in order to identify differences in the effects of the changes that could be due to variations in labor force participation across generations. For some of our analyses, we used a measure of income that adjusts to account for household size and economies of scale. The adjustment is made by dividing household benefit levels by a "family equivalence scale. "[5] We did this to facilitate comparisons between non-married persons and married persons, whose household income includes income from both spouses that can vary significantly between them.[6] We also evaluated the effect of modifications on individual benefit levels. In addition to evaluating changes in benefit levels resulting from each modification, we assessed changes in a variable in the model that serves as a proxy for poverty avoidance.[7] Consistent with our past work on Social Security reform, when simulating benefits we compared benefits under each reform to two hypothetical benchmark policy scenarios that would achieve 75-year solvency, one by only increasing payroll taxes (which simulates "promised benefits") and the other by only reducing benefits (which simulates "funded benefits").[8] However, unlike prior GAO work, for the purposes of this study, we evaluated certain specific individual modifications, rather than comprehensive reform packages. We did this in order to focus on modifications that account for more recent changes in family structure and labor force composition. Additionally, to facilitate comparisons across cohorts, we generally report the effect of each modification in terms of percent changes in benefit levels. Using such a measure, the outcomes from each benchmark are largely similar. In the body of the report, in most cases, we present output from simulations using the "promised benefits" benchmark. Detailed output from both benchmarks is presented in appendix II. For this report, we focused on examining the distribution of benefits and did not assess equity measures. While our simulations provide estimates of future retirement income, there is a considerable amount of uncertainty involved with these estimates. Since these estimates could change significantly, depending on assumptions used and behavioral responses, they should not be considered predictions.

We conducted our work between January 2006 and August 2007 in accordance with generally accepted government auditing standards. A more detailed discussion of our scope and methodology appears in appendix I.

RESULTS IN BRIEF

Generally, women have less retirement income than men, largely because of women's lower labor force attachment and lower earnings, on average. Fewer women than men have income from most major retirement sources, and those women who do receive income from these sources receive less than men. Women's median Social Security benefit is approximately 70 percent of the median benefit that men receive. Meanwhile, fewer women than men have pension incomes, and the median value of their pensions is about half that of men's. While only a small proportion of men and women aged 65 and over are engaged in the paid labor force, among those who are, women earn just over half of what men earn. While there is less distinction between the income of men and women from assets such as interest, dividends, rents, and royalties, women earn somewhat less than men from these sources as well. Not surprisingly, older women are more often poor than men. Among those 65 and over, 12 percent of women are in poverty, compared to 7 percent of men. Although women's work outside the home has increased substantially in the last century—with the labor force participation rate of married women aged 16 and over increasing from approximately 32 percent in 1960 to 61 percent in 2006—they spend fewer years in the labor force than men and they more often work part- time. Additionally, they tend to earn less than men during their working years, earning only 77 percent of what men earned for full-time, year- round work in 2005. Although work patterns are key in earnings differences, in prior work we found that even after accounting for these and other behavioral differences—such as educational attainment— women still earn less than men.

Certain life events—including changes in marital status, labor force interruptions, and long-term care needs— can significantly reduce the amount of pension income and Social Security benefits for both men and women. However, because of women's lower earnings and labor force participation, these events may increase the probability women will enter retirement with fewer financial resources than men. Divorce often results in economic loss for both men and women, but women tend to experience more economic loss than men. Further, at retirement, Social Security divorced-spouse benefits are available only if the marriage lasted at least 10 years. Women's role as primary family caregiver for children and elderly relatives can also reduce their career earnings. For example, one study documented that almost half of women who worked during pregnancy with their first child took unpaid leave and one-quarter quit their jobs. Because women tend to live longer than men, they are more likely than men to experience widowhood. Social Security income is reduced at the household level upon the death of a spouse, and widows do not often retain all of their husbands' pension benefits. In part because of their longer average life spans, with age, women are also more likely than men to become disabled and need long-term care, further increasing demand upon their retirement resources.

Our simulations of some proposed changes to the Social Security system and the employer-sponsored pension system resulted in different effects on women and men, and among different subgroups of women, because of differences in lifetime work histories. Some of the proposed changes to Social Security that we analyzed are in fact designed to increase the benefits of targeted groups by taking advantage of differences in workforce participation patterns. On one hand, our model results showed that modifications that compensate for low earnings or time spent out of the workforce for caregiving tend to increase benefits for beneficiaries overall, and particularly those in lower income quintiles. For example, when we simulated a dependent care credit to compensate for zero or low earnings when children are young, benefits increased across the board for women in all marital statuses and in all income quintiles. On the other hand, the changes that focus on shifts in family structure, such as increases in two-earner couples and increased incidence of divorce, tend to increase the benefits of groups targeted by the change, but produce mixed results for others. For example, our simulation of a reduction in Social Security's marriage eligibility rule had a narrowly focused impact on a very small number of women and almost no men. Some pension rule changes that have been proposed or passed into law in the past several years take into account changes in the labor force and the changing norms of employer-provided retirement plans; while these changes are gender-neutral, they may provide important new opportunities for some women to increase their retirement income. For example, when we simulated a pension change that would ensure that 100 percent of retirement account balances would roll over to another qualified account when individuals switched jobs (rather than allowing some or all of the balance to be withdrawn or spent), among those affected, women had larger median percentage changes than men, and among women, never-married and divorced women had the largest median percentage changes in pension income.

The departments of Labor and the Treasury and the Social Security Administration provided technical comments which we incorporated as appropriate.

BACKGROUND

The retirement outlook for both men and women in the United States has changed significantly in the last 30 years. Like many industrialized countries, the United States is undergoing a significant demographic shift toward an aging population and is experiencing the increased pressures on the social insurance, medical, and private pension systems that this shift creates.

While life expectancy in the United States has steadily increased over the last 50 years, birthrates have declined, and both have led to rapid growth in the proportion of the population comprised of elderly people: in 1950, those aged 65 or older made up 8 percent of the population; in 2000, this proportion rose to 12 percent and is projected to rise to almost 20 percent by 2030. Also, between 1940 and 1980, women's life expectancy generally increased faster than men's. During the same time period, the difference in life expectancy at age 65 for women and men grew from 1.5 years in 1940 to 4.4 years in 1980. (See figure 1.)

Source: Social Security Administration.

Note: Data for 2004 through 2006 are preliminary or estimated. The period life expectancy at a given age for a given year represents the average number of years of life remaining if a group of persons at that age were to experience the mortality rates for that year over the course of their remaining lives.

Figure 1. Life expectancy at age 65, 1940 to 2006 and projected 2007 to 2085.

The difference in men's and women's longevity has decreased over the past 25 years, and that difference is expected to remain stable throughout much of the 21st century. Nevertheless, the ratio of elderly women to elderly men increased substantially in the post-World War II era, and elderly women will continue to outnumber elderly men both in numbers and as a percent of the population for the foreseeable future. (See figure 2.) As a result of these trends, women can expect on average to spend more years in retirement than men.

Traditionally, the financial resources that provide retirement security have been characterized as a three-legged stool: Social Security, pensions, and savings, although increasingly, earnings are also a significant source of income for the elderly. Overall, women have been more likely than men to rely on Social Security to finance their retirement. Moreover, some aspects of the Social Security system particularly benefit women. For instance, because women tend to have lower lifetime taxable earnings than men, they benefit from the Social Security system's progressive benefit formula, which replaces a larger portion of lifetime earnings for people with low earnings than for people with high earnings. In addition, Social Security is designed specifically to accommodate both low- or non-earning spouses, often women, by providing them with a dependent benefit based upon their spouses' earnings. Social Security was created based upon the model of a single-earner married couple family structure, and while many women still never enter the paid workforce or choose to reduce their workforce participation, at least in part to care for children or other family members, the single-earner family model no longer describes the typical American household. Nevertheless, this structure has been and continues to be extremely beneficial to some women.

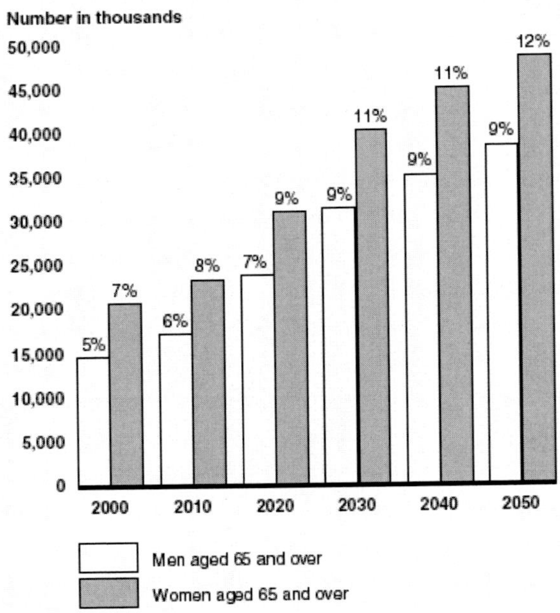

Source: U.S. Census Bureau, Demographic Trends of the 20th Century.
Note: Percentage values over each bar show the total U.S. population represented by each bar.

Figure 2. Men and women aged 65 and over: Number and percent of the total U.S. population, Projections 2000 to 2050.

However, Social Security faces a long-term financing shortfall resulting largely from longer life spans and lower birthrates. According to 2007 Social Security projections,[9] absent policy changes, Social Security tax revenue is expected to fall short of benefit payments for the first time in 2017; by 2041 the system may have inadequate resources to pay full benefits. As a result, in the future, Social Security's role could change. Reductions in scheduled benefits and/or increases in program revenues will be needed to restore the long-term solvency and sustainability of the program. Within the program's current structure, possible benefit changes might include changes to the benefit formula or reductions in cost-of-living increases, among other options; revenue increases might include increases in payroll taxes or transfers from the Treasury's general fund.[10] In addition, many proposals have been put forth over the past several decades to address the adequacy of Social Security benefits for different kinds of workers and their families. These proposals often address the needs of spouses, survivors, and low earners as well as those with significant workforce interruptions.

Additionally, many workers bear greater risk and responsibility for their retirement savings than in the past. About half of U.S. workers do not have a pension plan through their employer, and those who do are less likely than in the past to be covered by defined benefit (DB) plans. Among those who offer plans, employers have increasingly shifted from traditional DB to defined contribution (DC) plans, such as 401(k)s, which are based on contributions to and investment returns on individuals' accounts. While private sector DB plans must offer a guaranteed lifetime income in the form of an annuity, DC plans more often provide the beneficiary with a lump sum as the only option.[11] While individuals could take the proceeds of their lump sum and purchase an annuity, the cost of purchasing a private annuity may make this option unattractive to many households. In addition, the private equity market charges women a higher premium for a life annuity than it charges men of the same age, because on average women live longer than men.[12]

Personal savings have traditionally been an important source of retirement income. Unfortunately, despite the challenges facing both public and private benefit systems for the elderly, relatively few Americans are currently saving, and some research suggests that women have less in savings than men. According to some measures, America has the lowest overall saving rate of any major industrialized nation. The U.S personal saving rate as a percentage of disposable personal income has recently reached levels not seen since the Great Depression, falling below 1 percent in 2005 and 2006.[13] A variety of proposals seeking to encourage more individuals to save have been introduced in the past several years. Many of these proposals target low- and moderate-income workers who are least likely to have access to employer-sponsored pension plans. Some of these proposals create added incentives or ease access for individuals to save through existing savings vehicles, such as 401(k) plans or individual retirement accounts (IRA). Other plans would create new vehicles for savings, such as 40 1(k) type plans for those not currently covered by a plan. One mechanism that already exists to encourage individuals to save is the so-called spousal IRA offered to non-earning spouses, who are most often women, as a way to build retirement income. A spousal IRA, allows non-earning spouses to accumulate retirement savings in their own retirement accounts.[14]

Finally, health care coverage and rising health costs have added to the financial burden for retirees. Retired Americans often rely on employer- sponsored health benefits to provide health coverage until they become eligible for Medicare or to supplement their Medicare coverage. In 2005 about 37 percent of retirees were covered by such plans.[15] However, retirees are paying more for these benefits, and the number of private employers offering them has declined considerably.[16] The rate of growth of health care costs has generally outpaced the rate of U.S. economic growth, and this trend is likely to continue, jeopardizing the availability of employer-sponsored insurance for many. Rapidly rising health care costs may be particularly burdensome for retirees with limited financial resources. Additionally, the odds of having a disability or chronic illness increase with age; since, on average, women live longer, dealing with the cost of declining health may be a particular concern for women.

Women Have Less Retirement Income than Men Largely because of Differences in Labor Force Participation and Lifetime Earnings

Generally, women have less retirement income than men, largely because, on average, women have lower labor force attachment and lower earnings than men. While about 90 percent of men and women aged 65 and older receive Social Security benefits, fewer women than men have income from most other major sources of retirement income,[17] and they receive less than men from those sources, according to a Congressional Research Service analysis of Census Bureau data.[18] Additionally, women aged 65 and older have higher rates of poverty than men of the same age. While women's labor force participation has increased substantially in the last half century, it has flattened out in recent years and remains more intermittent than men's. Women also tend to earn less than men during their working years.

Women Have Less in Total Retirement Income than Men

While Social Security provides retirement income to almost 90 percent of all elderly people, a smaller percentage of women than men age 65 and older have additional income from pensions, assets—such as interest or dividends from lifetime savings, or earnings, according to the Congressional Research Service analysis of Census Bureau data.[19] For example, in 2004, the percentage of men with income from pensions was almost twice that of women and 44 percent more men than women had wage and salary income. (See figure 3.)

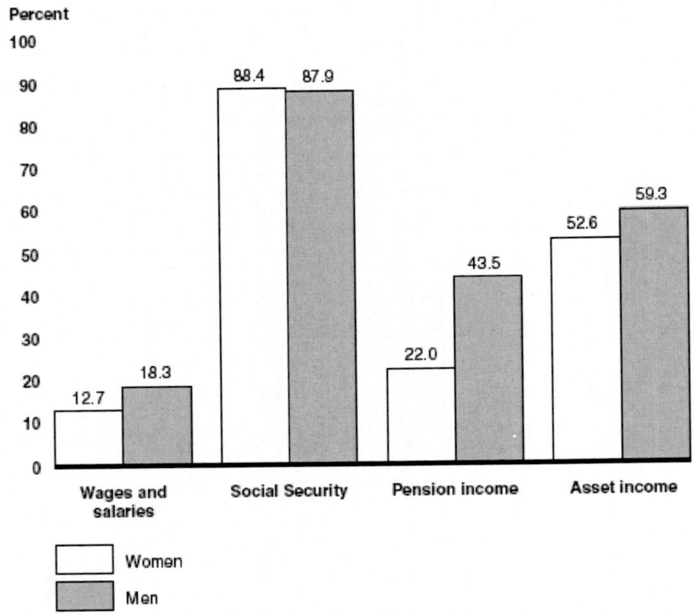

Source: Congressional Research Service analysis of the Census Bureau's Current Population Survey data.

Figure 3. Percentage of the population age 65 and older receiving income from various sources, 2004.

Moreover, women's median incomes from each of the various retirement sources are lower than men's. As shown in figure 4, men's median annual Social Security income was $12,583 in 2004, while women's was $8,799. Nevertheless, Social Security is an important financial resource for women, many of whom receive spousal, divorced spousal, or survivor benefits. According to the Social Security Administration (SSA), while Social Security is the largest single source of income for most of the elderly population age 65 and older, it represents 53 percent of total income for elderly unmarried women—including divorced, widowed, and never married women, compared to 38 percent for unmarried men. Moreover,

Social Security was nearly the only source of income for close to half of all elderly unmarried women who received it in 2004, compared to a little more than a third of elderly unmarried men. Importantly, Social Security can become a growing fraction of total retirement income over time since it is indexed to offset the effects of inflation. In contrast, private pensions and income from assets are rarely indexed. Unlike Social Security, pension income may end upon the death of the spouse if the retired worker elects to receive a single life annuity,[20] in which payments cease at the time of the worker's death.[21]

The difference between men's and women's pension income is larger than for Social Security. In 2004, men's median pension income was nearly twice women's, $12,000 and $6,141, respectively. Asset income is relatively low for both women and men compared to Social Security and pensions. Nevertheless, women's median asset income was $750, while men's was slightly higher at $964. Finally, while less than a fifth of the elderly had wage and salary earnings in 2004, men's median earnings were $20,800, while women's were $12,000. (See figure 4.)

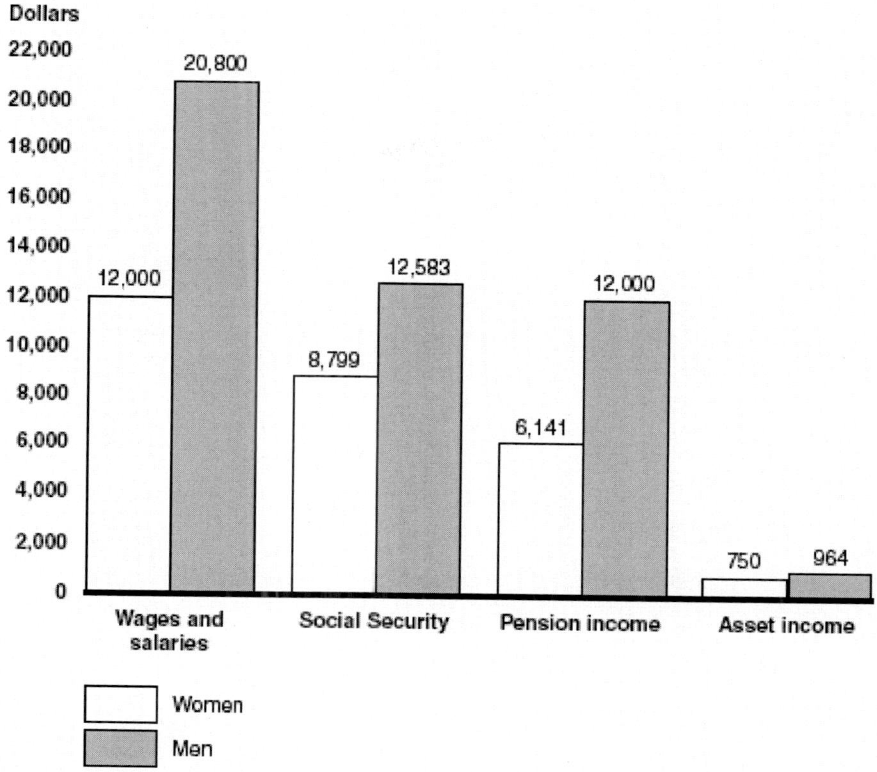

Source: Congressional Research Service analysis of the Census Bureau's Current Population Survey data.

Figure 4. Median annual income of the population age 65 and older, 2004.

Additionally, rates of poverty among those 65 and over are higher for women than for men.[22] Over time, overall poverty rates among the elderly have declined from 35 percent in 1959 to 10 percent in 2005, according to Census Bureau data. This is in part due to Social Security benefits for the aged. Here, too, gender differences remain. In 2004, 12 percent of women and 7 percent of men age 65 and older had incomes below the federal poverty level, with more pronounced variation among individuals of different marital status. For example, never-married elderly men and women had the highest rates of poverty, while the next highest rates were among divorced and widowed elderly women. Married couples had significantly lower rates than all other marital statuses. (See figure 5.) Moreover, almost 21 percent of women age 65 and older who lived alone were poor, in comparison to almost 15 percent of men who lived alone.

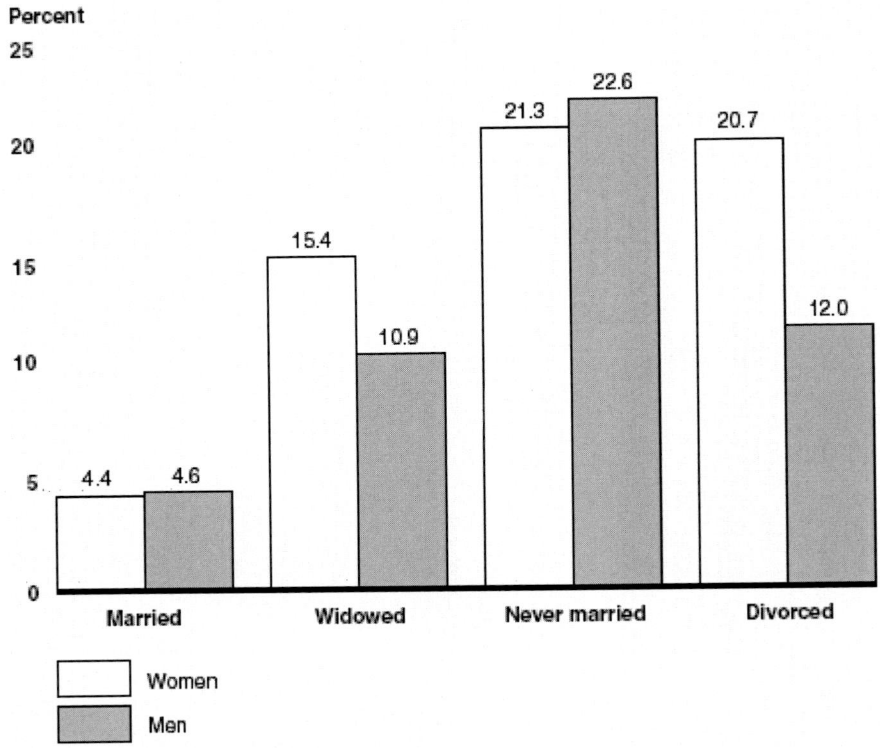

Source: Social Security Administration.

Figure 5. Poverty rates among people age 65 and older by marital status, 2004.

Women Have More Intermittent Work Histories and Lower Earnings than Men

Women's labor force participation increased substantially in the latter half of the 20th century, although women continue to work fewer total years than men and more often work part-time. While women's participation in the labor force increased from the mid-1960s through the late 1990s, men's labor force participation has steadily decreased, most significantly between the mid-1950s and the early-1970s.[23] (See figure 6.)

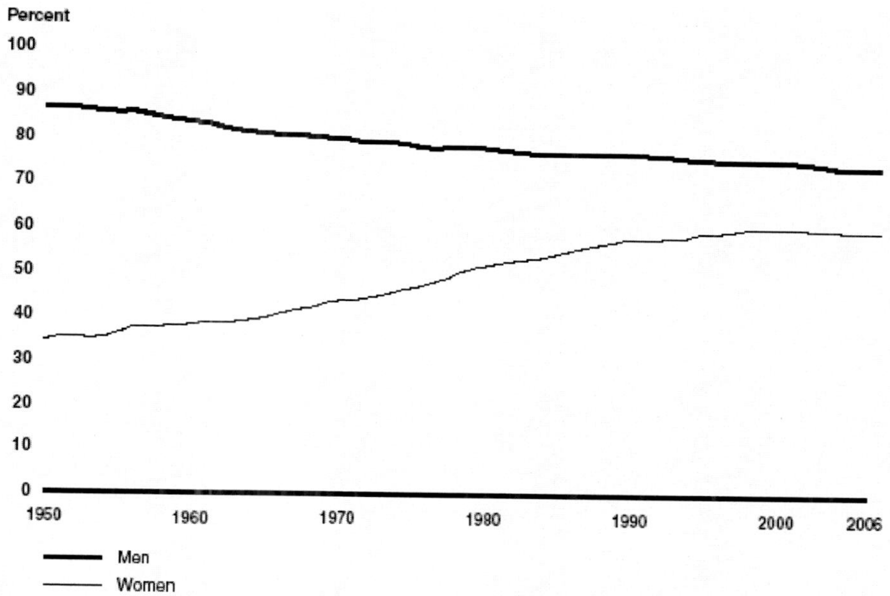

Source: U.S. Department of Labor, Bureau of Labor Statistics.

Figure 6. Overall labor force participation rate of men and women age 16 and older, 1950–2006.

Much of the change in women's participation rates is due to higher labor force participation rates among married women. According to Census Bureau statistics, between 1960 and 1995 married women's labor force participation increased from almost 32 to 61 percent and has not changed significantly in the past decade. As a result, there are now more married couple households with two earners than when Social Security was first established. These overall trends have recently stabilized, and in 2006 the Bureau of Labor Statistics predicted that women's labor force participation rate will not change significantly in the near future.[24]

Despite the overall increases in women's labor force participation, women continue to have more intermittent labor force participation than men. As we reported in 2003, women have fewer years of work experience, work fewer hours per year, are less likely to work a full-time schedule, and leave the labor force for longer periods of time than men.25 For example, [25] percent of women and almost 11 percent of men age 16 and older usually worked part-time in 2005.[26]

In addition to their spending less time in the workforce overall, women earn less than men when they are working.[27] Although women's earnings have risen relative to men's over time, women nevertheless continue to earn less than men. According to Census Bureau data, in 2005, women earned 77 percent of what men earned for full-time, year-round work. (See figure 7.)

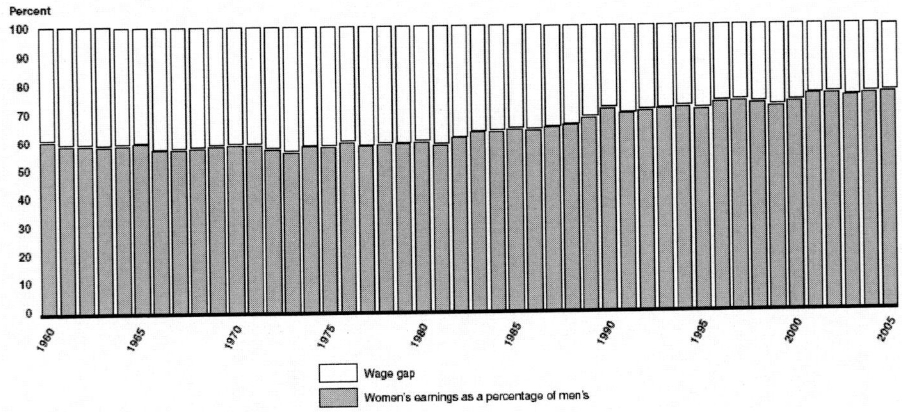

Source: U.S. Census Bureau.

Note: Based on median earnings of full-time, year-round workers 15 years old and over. Before 1989 earnings are for civilian workers only.

Figure 7. Women's median earnings for full-time, year-round work as a percentage of men's, 1960 to 2005.

This difference may be due, in part, to the fact that women continue to take primary responsibility for family care and those who work outside the home may trade some career advancement for schedule flexibility. In fact, in prior work we found that work patterns are a key factor in explaining the differences in men's and women's earnings. However, even after accounting for these and other behavioral factors—such as educational attainment—unexplained differences remained.[28]

Changes in women's labor force participation have also increased their participation in employer-provided pension plans, according to one study,[29] though, as noted earlier, their overall rates of participation are still lower than men's. Women who worked full-time throughout the year actually had higher pension participation rates than men with similar work schedules in 2005,[30] but women's overall rates remain lower because, in part, of their lower rate of full-time work and lower earnings, according to the Employee Benefit Research Institute. While the increase suggests that a larger share of women in younger cohorts will likely qualify for pensions based on their own earnings, many women may continue to receive spousal or survivor benefits through their husbands' pensions. In addition, the general shift from DB to DC plans may have both positive and negative consequences for women. Women may especially benefit from the greater portability afforded by DC plans because of their more intermittent labor force participation. However, another consequence of this general shift is that with many DC plans, individuals have a greater responsibility to make prudent investment decisions and to make their retirement savings last over their lifetimes, which for women, on average, are longer than for men.

Changes in women's labor force participation have also increased the percentage of women who are insured under Social Security based on their own work history, even though many women continue to receive dependent benefits as spouses. According to SSA, women who were eligible to receive benefits based on their own work records increased from 22 percent to 84 percent between 1950 and 2006. Nevertheless, in December of 2005, approximately 60 percent of retired women received Social Security benefits based, at least in part, on their marital history.[31] Moreover, nearly all spousal and survivor beneficiaries were women in 2005. Further, as women's labor force participation increases, many will find that benefits based on their own work records are more generous than the spousal benefit. However, when many of these same women become widows, they will likely begin to collect benefits based on their marital status, as the survivor's benefit, at 100 percent of their deceased spouse's benefit, is likely to be greater than their own.

Data on current retirees reflect the fact that those retirees comprise older generations of workers, in which women's labor force participation rates were lower than those of current workers. In the future, data that include later generations of women, with greater labor force participation rates, may show greater percentages of women eligible for and collecting benefits based on their own work records. Nevertheless, the key factor contributing to the difference in men's and women's Social Security income levels will continue to be the difference in their lifetime work histories and earnings. Women's continued intermittent labor force participation and lower median earnings than men's result in lower benefit amounts, even though Social Security replaces a greater percentage of preretirement earnings for lower-wage workers.[32]

Certain Life Events May Reduce Women's Retirement Resources More than Men's

Certain life events— including changes in marital status, labor force interruptions, and long-term care needs— can significantly reduce the amount of pension income and Social Security benefits for both men and women. However, because of women's lower earnings and labor force participation, these events may exacerbate the deficiency of women's financial resources in retirement. Divorce often results in economic loss for both men and women, but women tend to experience more economic loss than men. In addition, women are most often the family members who provide unpaid care, which can reduce their career earnings as well. The death of a spouse can also reduce retirement income for the survivor, and because they generally live longer, women have higher rates of widowhood than men at older ages. While declining health at older ages has significant implications for both men's and women's financial security, because of life expectancy differences, women more often require costly long-term care assistance.

Divorce May Reduce Women's Retirement Income

Research has shown that married couples generally have greater household wealth than nonmarried men and women and that marital disruption negatively affects both men's and women's economic statuses.[33] While divorce may result in a reduced standard of living for both men and women, divorced women, as a group, experience more economic loss than divorced men.[34] For example, the Census Bureau reported that in 2001, 23 percent of recently divorced women, in comparison to nearly 8 percent of recently divorced men, had income below the poverty level.[35] One study found that marital disruption, including divorce, resulted in a substantial drop in women's income and loss of assets.[36] Another study projected in 2000 that most divorced women are more likely than never-married,

married, and widowed women to be in the bottom 40 percent of the income distribution at age 67.[37] As shown in figure 5, elderly divorced women have higher rates of poverty, at over 20 percent, than elderly divorced men, at 12 percent.

In retirement, divorce has the potential to reduce Social Security benefits because Social Security's eligibility rules require that the marriage last at least 10 years for a divorced spouse to claim benefits from an ex-spouse's earnings record.[38] However, Census Bureau data from 2001 show that more than half of first and second marriages that ended in divorce lasted less than 10 years.[39]

Unlike Social Security benefits, divorced spouses can, under certain circumstances, receive all or part of their former spouses' private pension benefits, regardless of the marriage's duration. Although the Employee Retirement Income Security Act of 1974 (ERISA)[40] generally does not allow workers to assign their benefits to another person in this way, Congress amended the law in 1984 through the Retirement Equity Act (REA)[41] to permit the payment of pension benefits to a worker's former spouse under a qualified domestic relations order (QDRO). A QDRO, which meets certain statutory requirements, including approval by a court and the plan administrator, may be used to satisfy certain obligations, such as child support, alimony, or the division of marital property.[42] However, the worker's pension benefits may be reduced. Additionally, women often forgo the protection provided by QDRO's. This may happen for a variety of reasons, in some cases women may be unaware that their spouses are covered by a pension, while others may not know that they can receive benefits while their spouses are alive.

Family Caregiving, which Can Reduce Lifetime Earnings, Is More Common for Women than for Men

Family caregiving, which encompasses important child care and elder care responsibilities, is more often provided by women. In order to meet these family needs, some caregivers reduce work hours or leave the labor force altogether. For example, one Census Bureau study shows that 45 percent of women who worked during pregnancy with their first child between 1996 and 2000 took unpaid leave and one-quarter quit their job.[43] Bureau of Labor Statistics data indicate that, among parents with children under age 6, almost 92 percent of fathers, compared to over 58 percent of mothers, were employed in 2005.[44] Research shows that in addition to caring for children, women provide unpaid care for a family member or friend more often than men. In 2002, daughters or daughters-in-law provided care to frail, older adults living in the community more often than sons or sons-inlaw, according to one study.[45] Similarly, another study found that employed women were more likely than employed men to provide care for a child, spouse, or partner with a disability.[46] Finally, one study reported that wives tend to reduce their work hours when a husband experiences a severe health shock, such as a stroke.[47]

Caregiving can negatively affect the provider's career earnings and, consequently, retirement income. Although many caregivers are employed, research shows that caregivers can experience substantial losses in career development and workforce earnings as well as significant out-of-pocket expenses.[48] For example, one study showed that women age 46 and older who began caregiving for elderly relatives between 1987 and 1992 experienced an average of over $3,000 loss in annual earnings.[49] Another study showed that over half of caregivers who worked while providing care reported that this role required them to adjust their work schedules, such as arriving late, or even quit work. Furthermore, years spent out of the paid labor force can reduce a worker's Social Security benefit amount. Moreover, one study found that caregiving for adult parents can raise women's risk of poverty in later years.[50]

Women Are More Likely to Experience Widowhood, which Puts Them at Risk for Poverty

Older women are several times more likely than older men to experience widowhood. For example, in 2004 women age 65 and older were as likely to be widowed as married, while men were 5.5 times more likely to be married than widowed. (See figure 8.)

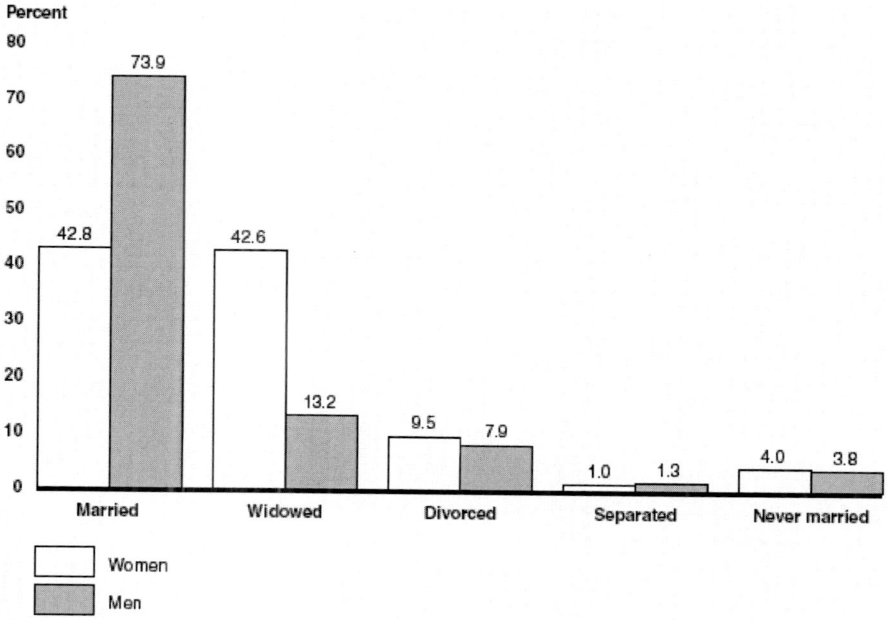

Source: U.S. Census Bureau.
Note: "Married" refers to now married, except separated.

Figure 8. Marital status of the population age 65 and older, 2005.

Despite changes to the Social Security system in the 1970s that improved widows' financial outcomes, research shows that widows continue to be at risk for poverty in old age.[51] As noted earlier, widows age 65 and older had over three times the poverty rate of married women or men in 2004. Widowhood may cause Social Security and pension income to decrease at the household level, which can be a hardship if certain fixed costs, such as housing, remain the same. More specifically, household Social Security income is reduced by one-third if the couple's benefits had been based on one spouse's work history and by up to 50 percent if both spouses had been receiving retired worker benefits.[52] In addition, pension income is likely to be reduced for the surviving spouse.

The REA helped protect spouses and widows by requiring employers to obtain a spouse's written consent in order for a worker to decline the joint and survivor annuity default option. A common default for the joint and survivor annuity provides a 50 percent benefit level to the surviving spouse. However, the shift from DB pension plans to DC pension plans has the potential to provide even less income security for widows who rely on a spouse's pension income. Although DC plans generally must provide that an employee's vested account balance is payable in full on death to the surviving spouse, the employee may, during his or her lifetime, make withdrawals from the account or roll over the balance into an IRA without spousal consent.

Simulated Retirement Income for Women with Varying Workforce Attachment and Marital Status

To illustrate the potential impact of workforce attachment and marital status on women's retirement income, we used the Policy Simulation Group's retirement income models to estimate Social Security and pension income for individuals in a sample of a simulated 1985 birth cohort at ages 67 and 85. The Policy Simulation Group's model incorporates information on the estimated effects of various factors on retirement income and is useful for illustrating potential differences in outcome under the current policy environment. (For a discussion of limitations of the model, see app. I.)

The simulation projected that women who worked full-time for 36 or more years would have median annual Social Security benefits of nearly $25,000 at age 67, while those who worked full-time between 1 and 5 years had a median annual benefit of about $13,000. In another example, median annual pension benefits for women who worked full-time for 36 or more years were almost $21,000, while median pension benefits among women with 1 to 5 years of full-time work were less than $900.

The simulation also projected that among those who had worked for at least 36 years, married women's median Social Security benefits were over $26,000 at age 67 and widow's benefits were slightly lower. Median benefit levels for divorced women were nearly $22,000 and for never married women, just over $20,000. Also, median Social Security benefit levels for women in our simulated sample who were married and worked between 1 and 5 years were nearly $17,000, while those of never married women with similar work histories were not quite $9,000.

Among women who worked for at least 36 years, the simulation projected that married women's median pension benefits were about $19,000 at age 67 and widow's benefits were just over $24,000. Median benefit levels for divorced women were over $21,000, and for never married women, over $20,000. In addition, median pension benefit levels for women in our simulated sample who were married and worked full-time between 1 and 5 years were over $2,000, while those of never married or divorced women who had worked full-time between 1 and 5 years in general did not have any pension income.

Source: GAO analysis of GEMINI and PENSIM data.
Note: All dollar values are in 2007 dollars.

Health Care Costs May Deplete Elderly Women's Retirement Resources

Declining health at older ages has significant implications for women's financial security. At least in part because women have longer average life spans than men, women are more likely than men to become disabled and need long-term care as they age. In 2003, among Medicare enrollees age 65 and older, more women than men reported an inability to perform at least one of five certain physical functions, such as the ability to walk two to three blocks.[53] Women are significantly more likely than men to develop severe disabilities, and one study estimated that women age 65 have a 44 percent chance of entering a nursing home, compared to 27 percent for men.[54] Women represented 72 percent of all nursing home residents in 1999 and 70 percent of home care consumers in 2000.[55] Research shows that nursing home entry has important financial consequences for the elderly, especially for unmarried women.[56] In 2006, Genworth Financial estimated that the average annual cost for nursing home care was $70,912 and for assisted living facilities, $32,294.[57] In addition, out-of-pocket medical costs during the last years of a spouse's life can deplete the couple's resources substantially and contribute to poverty among surviving spouses, who are most often widows.[58]

Specific Changes to Social Security and Employer-Sponsored Pensions Will Affect Women Differently than Men Because of Differences in Lifetime Work Histories

The specific changes to Social Security and pensions that we modeled had different effects on women and men, and among different subgroups of women, because of differences in lifetime work histories. Some of the proposed modifications to Social Security that we analyzed are in fact designed to increase the benefits of targeted groups by accounting for differences in workforce participation patterns. On one hand, our model results showed that modifications that compensate for low earnings or time spent out of the workforce for caregiving tend to increase benefits for beneficiaries overall, and particularly those in lower income quintiles. On the other hand, our results showed that modifications that focus on changes in family structure, such as more two-earner couples and an increased incidence of divorce, tend to increase the benefits of groups targeted by the change, but produce mixed results for others. A number of pension modifications proposed in the last several years take into account changes in the labor force and the changing norms of employer-provided retirement plans; while these reforms are gender-neutral, they may provide important new opportunities for women to increase their retirement income.

While the costs associated with each of the Social Security program modifications modeled in this report vary, all but one[59] would have a negative effect on trust fund solvency regardless of the benchmark used. Because we have analyzed each modification in isolation, we present the solvency impact for each modification in isolation; as part of a larger package of reforms, the solvency impact of each change may vary. For a summary of the solvency impact of each simulated change under both the "promised benefits" and "funded benefits" benchmarks, see appendix IV. For more information on both the "promised benefits" and the "funded benefits" benchmark, see appendix I.

System Modifications Designed to Increase Social Security Benefits for Specific Populations Do So, but Sometimes Only Marginally

Using the Policy Simulation Group's GEMINI and SSASIM models,[60] we assessed the effects of certain specific modifications that were designed to enhance Social Security benefits for specific subgroups of beneficiaries at age 70.[61] We used both a family equivalence scale and individual level analysis to be able to both compare between married and unmarried individuals and to assess the impact of modifications on individuals alone. Each of the changes discussed below increases benefits for the targeted group, but the size of the increase projected varies with the number of people affected; generally, the smaller the population that was targeted by the reform, the larger the change in benefits and vice versa. While some of the individual modifications modeled below have no benefit impact outside of the targeted group, for those that do have broader effects, the impact on other beneficiaries can vary. The results of our analyses reflect outcomes for individuals in the simulated populations and do not attempt to estimate outcomes for an actual population.

Implement Dependent Care Credits

Dependent care credit proposals seek to compensate those who spend some years out of the workforce to care for dependents or those with low or reduced earnings while attending to caregiving responsibilities. Fewer years in the workforce or reduced earnings during caregiving years tend to lower a caregiver's average lifetime earnings and, thus, his or her Social Security benefit levels in retirement. Many advocates have proposed dependent care proposals that either modify Social Security's traditional benefit formula, which uses a 35-year span of time to average lifetime earnings or credit caregivers with additional earnings. These proposals vary in design and do not necessarily produce similar results. Either option would require data collection and computation beyond SSA's current practices, a potential administrative complication.

- **Specified earnings credit:** This approach would assign to the caregiver one half of average earnings for each year in which there was a child in care and the actual earning was zero or reduced from prior earnings for a fixed number of years. Those who already earn the credit amount would not benefit. Research has shown that a caregiver credit model based on crediting earnings does a better job of targeting lower earners than excluding care years from earning averages.[62]
- **Excluding care years from earning averages:** This approach would reduce the standard 35-year basis for determining a worker's average indexed monthly earnings by subtracting the number of years spent providing care. It generally also specifies a limit for the number of years that can be dropped from the calculation of average earnings. Because the design specifies years of zero earnings, this approach may not target financially needy populations who lack sufficient resources to take full years off from work. High-income caregivers may be more likely to benefit from such an approach if economic necessity drives low-income caregivers back to the workforce, while those in highincome families are able to stay out of the workforce longer.

GAO Simulation of a Dependent Care Credit

We simulated the effect of a dependent care credit similar to one evaluated by the Urban Institute[63] that would credit a worker's earnings record with one-half of average wages in years in which there was a child under 5 years of age[64] in the household and the worker's earnings were less than one half of average wages.[65] We evaluated the impact on the Social Security benefits of two simulated populations—one cohort born in 1950 and another born in 1985.[66]

Using the GEMINI model, we found that this particular dependent care credit resulted in positive median benefit changes for both women and men, though it provided a larger increase in median benefits for women. The credit was more beneficial for those born in 1950 than in 1985. As shown in table 1, its outcome was progressive for those affected by the change, with women in the lowest earnings quintile showing the highest proportionate gain in their Social Security benefits. In both cohorts, nevermarried women had the largest median change in benefits.[67] The effect of this change was also broad; for both birth cohorts, it affected the largest number of beneficiaries, both men and women, of any of our simulations.

Table 1. Median Percentage Change in Benefits for Individuals Whose Benefits Changed after Addition of the Dependent Care Credit—Promised Benefits Benchmark

Numbers in percent					
Birth cohort	All men			All women	
1950	2.60			3.24	
1985	2.06			2.63	
Women by income quintile					
Birth cohort	Lowest quintile	Quintile 2	Middle quintile	Quintile 4	Highest quintile
1950	7.96	4.16	2.80	1.68	0.92
1985	6.88	3.50	2.12	1.14	0.72
Women by marital status					
Birth cohort		Never married	Divorced	Married	Widowed
1950		7.95	5.05	2.64	2.87
1985		6.69	4.18	2.19	2.43

Source: GAO analysis based on the GEMINI model.

Note: Simulations calculated benefits for individuals at age 70 and were based on benefits adjusted for household size (for more information, see discussion of Family Equivalence Scale in appendix I). Income quintiles are based on the distribution of the present value of family lifetime earnings for the whole population (male and female). For percentage of population affected and results using the "Funded benefits" benchmark, see appendix II.

Table 2. Percentage of Total Simulation Population Whose Benefits Changed after Addition of the Dependent Care Credit—Promised Benefits Benchmark

Numbers in percent		
	Birth Cohort	
	1950	1985
All men	28.43	35.06
All women	30.93	30.99

Source: GAO analysis based on the GEMINI model.

Note: Simulations calculated benefits for individuals at age 70 and were based on benefits adjusted for household size (for more information, see discussion of Family Equivalence Scale in appendix I).

INCREASE MINIMUM BENEFIT

Minimum benefit proposals aim to ensure Social Security benefit adequacy for low earners. Under current law, Social Security includes a Special Primary Insurance Amount (also referred to as the Special Minimum Benefit) intended to reduce poverty among retired lifetime low-wage workers. The Special Primary Insurance Amount targets retirees with a low benefit based on a steady, long-time, low wage work record, rather than on those with a low benefit based on intermittent workforce attachment;[68] the Special Primary Insurance Amount makes this distinction by basing the calculation on years worked rather than earnings level. Very few people currently receive benefits based on the Special Primary Insurance Amount; however, the majority of those who do are women. Additionally, the benefit provided by the Special Primary Insurance Amount is less than the official poverty level for aged persons, and because the benefit is indexed to price inflation rather than wage growth, it has provided a less generous benefit over time relative to the traditional wage-indexed Social Security benefit. Because of this, SSA has projected that the Special Primary Insurance Amount will phase out as early as 2013. A newly designed minimum benefit could expand benefits for low earners across all demographic groups, including women, who are more likely than men to be at the bottom of the income distribution. Expanded minimum benefits may also be of renewed importance to benefit adequacy as part of a broad Social Security reform scenario that reduces benefits for all beneficiaries, including low earners.

Several Social Security reform proposals include a new minimum benefit that would guarantee a benefit equal to a set percentage of the poverty level, dependent on the number of years worked across a lifetime. For example, Estimated OASDI Financial Effects of the "Bipartisan Retirement Security Act of 2005"—legislation introduced as H.R. 440 by Representative Jim Kolbe and Representative Allen Boyd would provide low earners who had 40 years of minimum wage earnings a benefit equal to 120 percent of the federal poverty level when fully phased in.[69]

GAO Simulation of an Increased Minimum Benefit

To simulate the effect of an increased minimum benefit, we modeled a change to set a minimum benefit of 120 percent of the federal poverty level for 30-year workers, linearly phased to zero for workers with 20 years or less of covered employment. Slightly fewer men than women in the simulation were affected by the change, and those who were had a slightly lower median benefit changes than women affected by the change. As expected, the outcome of this change was largely progressive. In both cohorts, a larger share of women in the lower two income quintiles had benefit changes resulting from this modification than women in the upper three income quintiles.[70] Moreover, the median percentage changes in benefits for women in the bottom quintile was much larger than those for women in the higher quintiles. (See table 3.)

Table 3. Median Percentage Change in Benefits for Individuals Whose Benefits Changed after Addition of the Increased Minimum Benefit—Promised Benefits Benchmark

Numbers in percent					
Birth cohort		All men		All women	
1950		8.47		9.89	
1985		6.20		6.70	
Women by income quintile					
Birth cohort	Lowest quintile	Quintile 2	Middle quintile	Quintile 4	Highest quintile
1950	22.83	9.65	5.21	3.51	2.55
1985	8.26	2.45	2.27	0.09	0
Women by marital status					
Birth cohort	Never married	Divorced	Married	Widowed	
1950	22.80	17.13	7.43	8.34	
1985	19.01	14.50	4.55	6.48	

Source: GAO analysis based on the GEMINI model.

Note: Simulations calculated benefits for individuals at age 70 and were based on benefits adjusted for household size (for more information, see discussion of Family Equivalence Scale in appendix I). Income quintiles are based on the distribution of the present value of family lifetime earnings for the whole population (male and female). For percentage of population affected and results using the "Funded benefits" benchmark, see appendix II.

While the share of women affected by the minimum benefit was fairly similar across marital statuses (never-married, divorced, married and widowed) in each cohort (for data, see app. II, table 30), never-married and divorced women had much larger percent changes in median benefits. For never married women affected by the modification, the percent change in median benefits was more than double under the minimum benefit than under any other modification.[71]

Table 4. Percentage of Total Simulation Population Whose Benefits Changed after Addition of the Increased Minimum Benefit—Promised Benefits Benchmark

Numbers in percent		
	Birth Cohort	
	1950	1985
All men	7.71	8.77
All women	1.18	1.28

Source: GAO analysis based on the GEMINI model.

Note: Simulations calculated benefits for individuals at age 70 and were based on benefits adjusted for household size (for more information, see discussion of Family Equivalence Scale in appendix I).

The impact of the minimum benefit is larger in the 1950 cohort versus the 1985 cohort because the minimum benefit is linked to the poverty line, which is indexed to prices, while Social Security initial benefits are indexed to wages; over time, this results in a lower minimum benefit relative to Social Security benefits. This effect could be reduced by indexing the poverty level to wages rather than prices, as was done in the Kolbe-Boyd proposal.

A minimum benefit following parameters such as we simulated may increase benefits for both part-time and full-time workers. Because Social Security only tracks annual earnings rather than wages or hours worked, a higher-earning, part-time worker could receive the same benefit as a full-year, low-income worker; enhanced benefits may therefore also be provided to individuals who work part-time by choice.[72]

INCREASE SURVIVOR BENEFITS

One way that some proposals address the vulnerability of widows or widowers to poverty is by raising survivor benefits to a set percentage of a married couple's prior combined benefit (for example, two-thirds or threefourths of the level of benefits received by the couple while both were living). Under current law, a survivor receives the larger of his or her own benefit or the benefit of the deceased spouse. Thus, survivor benefits for many dually entitled women or women receiving only spousal benefits would replace approximately 67 percent of the couple's prior total benefit level. Researchers have expressed concern about whether this decline in total household benefits is too large to maintain the survivor's previous standard of living. On the other hand, for survivors of two-earner couples where both spouses received retired worker benefits on their own record, a widow's benefit under current law may range between 50 percent and 67 percent of the couple's prior total benefits upon the death of a spouse, causing an even greater decline in total household benefit income.

GAO Simulation of an Increased Survivor Benefit

GAO modeled a survivor benefit that would provide a surviving spouse with the higher of 75 percent of the couple's previous combined benefit level, capped at the average benefit level for all new retirees, or the current law survivor benefit. We did not simulate the effect of the current provision ensuring surviving spouses a minimum of 82.5 percent of the deceased worker's PIA; had this been included, results may be slightly higher. This simulation resulted in increased benefits for both men and women. (See table 5.) While about three times the number of women as men were affected, the magnitude of the benefit change was larger for men who were affected by the program modification; their median percentage change in benefits was nearly 29 percent in both cohorts. This is attributable to the increased survivor benefit modification compared to current law. Current law allows survivors the greater of their own benefit or their spouse's benefit. As most men receive a larger benefit than their spouses, a survivor benefit of the larger of 75 percent of the couple's combined benefit (capped at the average benefit level for all new retirees) or the husband's benefit would provide a higher benefit level than current law to lower-earning men who outlive their wives.

Table 5. Median Percentage Change in Benefits for Individuals Whose Benefits Changed after Addition of Increased Survivor Benefits—Promised Benefits Benchmark

Numbers in percent					
Birth cohort		All men		All women	
1950		28.78		15.71	
1985		28.98		8.36	
Women by income quintile					
Birth cohort	Lowest quintile	Quintile 2	Middle quintile	Quintile 4	Highestquintile
1950	14.81	16.28	15.77	13.69	24.44
1985	19.39	18.36	16.00	16.00	8.67
Women by marital status					
Birth cohort	Never married	Divorced	Married	Widowed	
1950	0	16.67	0	15.58	
1985	0	18.42	0	18.35	

Source: GAO analysis based on the GEMINI model.

Note: Simulations calculated benefits for individuals at age 70 and were based on benefits adjusted for household size (for more information, see discussion of Family Equivalence Scale in appendix I). Income quintiles are based on the distribution of the present value of family lifetime earnings for the whole population (male and female). For percentage of population affected and results using the "Funded benefits" benchmark, see appendix II.

Table 6. Percentage of Total Simulation Population Whose Benefits Changed after Addition of Increased Survivor Benefits—Promised Benefits Benchmark

Numbers in percent		
	Birth Cohort	
	1950	1985
All men	0.78	0.46
All women	2.11	1.13

Source: GAO analysis based on the GEMINI model.

Note: Simulations calculated benefits for individuals at age 70 and were based on benefits adjusted for household size (for more information, see discussion of Family Equivalence Scale in appendix I).

In both the 1985 and 1950 cohorts, the increased survivor benefit modification increased the number of women who never fell below the microsimulation model's low benefit threshold by about 6 percentage points versus current law. For those women affected by the benefit in our simulation, the median percentage change in benefits was about 16 percent in the 1950 cohort and about 18 percent in the 1985 cohort.[73] As expected, for both cohorts, the majority of women with benefit changes resulting from this change are widows and divorced women. Additionally, in terms of number of people affected, the impacts of this change were concentrated primarily in the bottom two income quintiles.[74] By capping this program modification at the level of average benefits, this modification targets the increased survivor's benefit to lower-earning widows and widowers. Although exempting wealthier beneficiaries from this benefit enhancement creates fiscal savings, it may limit many survivors from two-earner couples from benefiting from the change.

Reduce Spousal Benefits and Increase Survivor Benefits

An increase in survivor benefits is sometimes paired with a decrease in spousal benefits, from one-half the retired worker's benefit to one-third. This pairing provides nearly the same average percentage change in benefits to widows as the modification above, but contains costs by reducing the spousal benefit while the worker is still living.

GAO Simulation of a Reduction in Spousal Benefits with Increased Survivor Benefits

Table 7. Median Percentage Change in Benefits for Individuals Whose Benefits Changed after Addition of Decreased Spousal Benefits Paired with Increased Survivor Benefits—Promised Benefits Benchmark

Numbers in percent					
Birth cohort		All men		All women	
1950		-2.81		-2.66	
1985		-9.14		-8.78	
Women by income quintile					
Birth cohort	Lowest quintile	Quintile 2	Middle quintile	Quintile 4	Highestquintile
1950	-2.55	-2.55	-2.66	-2.67	-2.67
1985	-9.82	-8.06	-8.21	-8.45	-9.27
Women by marital status					
Birth cohort		Never married	Divorced	Married	Widowed
1950		0	-8.00	-2.67	15.58
1985		0	-24.11	-9.01	18.91

Source: GAO analysis based on the GEMINI model.

Note: Simulations calculated benefits for individuals at age 70 and were based on benefits adjusted for household size (for more information, see discussion of Family Equivalence Scale in appendix I). Income quintiles are based on the distribution of the present value of family lifetime earnings for the whole population (male and female). For percentage of population affected and results using the "Funded benefits" benchmark, see appendix II.

Our simulation of this modification resulted in nearly the same benefit changes for widows as the "Increase survivor benefits" projection described above, while the benefits of affected married women and divorced women—recipients of spousal benefits—had a generally negative change. When all women affected by this modification are sorted into quintiles by lifetime household income, the median percentage change in benefit levels is similar across quintiles, and is in all cases negative. (See table 7.) Despite this, the low benefit avoidance rates were quite similar to those produced by the survivor benefit increase modification for all cohorts, indicating that both modifications have nearly the same positive impact on our proxy for poverty avoidance (see app. III).

This proposal would both smooth household benefit levels before and after widowhood and provide savings to the Social Security system to offset costs of the increased survivor benefit.[75]

Table 8. Percentage of Total Simulation Population Whose Benefits Changed after Addition of Decreased Spousal Benefits Paired with Increased Survivor Benefits—Promised Benefits Benchmark

Numbers in percent		
	Birth Cohort	
	1950	1985
All men	11.45	11.58
All women	11.78	11.31

Source: GAO analysis based on the GEMINI model.

Note: Simulations calculated benefits for individuals at age 70 and were based on benefits adjusted for household size (for more information, see discussion of Family Equivalence Scale in appendix I).

Reduce Duration of Marriage Requirement for Divorced Spouse Benefit Eligibility

Proposals to shorten the current requirement for 10-year marriage duration to be eligible for divorced spouse and survivor benefits would expand eligibility for benefits to divorced spouses from marriages that do not meet the 10-year milestone.[76] Timing of divorce can have a large impact on retirement benefits, as an individual divorced one day before the 10 year anniversary would not be eligible for benefits, while another individual who waited one more day would be eligible for a full spousal or survivor benefit. Reducing the 10-year marriage requirement would make more divorced individuals eligible for divorced spouse and survivor benefits but would also increase the probability that an individual with several former spouses could have several spouses receive benefits on one worker's earnings record.

GAO Simulation of a Reduced Marriage Requirement

GAO simulated a modification that would reduce the duration of marriage requirement for receiving divorced spouse benefits from 10 to 7 years.[77] In the 1950 and 1985 cohorts, among women who had a benefit change due to the reduced marriage requirement, the median percentage change in benefits was about 65 percent and 45 percent respectively (see table 9), the largest median change in benefits for women among all reforms modeled. The scope of impact, however, was extremely small: In both cohorts, those affected made up less than 1 percent of the model sample.

Table 9. Median Percentage Change in Benefits for Individuals Whose Benefits Changed after Reduction in Marriage Requirement from 10 to 7 Years—Promised Benefits Benchmark

Numbers in percent					
Birth cohort		All men		All women	
1950		0.85		65.32	
1985		37.22		45.05	
Women by income quintile					
Birth cohort	Lowest quintile	Quintile 2	Middle quintile	Quintile 4	Highestquintile
1950	85.18	54.66	162.36	33.33	0
1985	53.99	34.41	33.33	36.31	25.14
Women by marital status					
Birth cohort	Never married	Divorced	Married	Widowed	
1950	0	65.32	0	0	
1985	0	45.05	0	0	

Source: GAO analysis based on the GEMINI model.

Note: Simulations calculated benefits for individuals at age 70 and were based on benefits adjusted for household size (for more information, see discussion of Family Equivalence Scale in appendix I). Income quintiles are based on the distribution of the present value of family lifetime earnings for the whole population (male and female). For percentage of population affected and results using the "Funded benefits" benchmark, see appendix II.

Table 10. Percentage of Total Simulation Population Whose Benefits Changed after Reduction in Marriage Requirement from 10 to 7 Years—Promised Benefits Benchmark

Numbers in percent		
	Birth Cohort	
	1950	1985
All men	0	0.03
All women	0.04	0.51

Source: GAO analysis based on the GEMINI model.

Note: Simulations calculated benefits for individuals at age 70 and were based on benefits adjusted for household size (for more information, see discussion of Family Equivalence Scale in appendix I).

The changes in this simulation also resulted in a handful of newly eligible beneficiaries: In the 1950 cohort, three individuals who were not previously eligible for Social Security benefits became eligible under the reform scenario, and in the 1985 cohort, 43 individuals became eligible. Among the seven simulations that we ran, this was the only one that resulted in new beneficiaries. This is because individuals who were not eligible on their record became eligible as spouses or survivors under the shorter duration of marriage requirement. These newly eligible beneficiaries are not included in the median percent change measures.

Pension Modifications that Address the Changing Pension Landscape and Changing Workforce Patterns May Serve Women Better than Traditional Pension Models

In addition to the Social Security proposal elements above, we simulated two pension modifications that address challenges related to the shift to DC plans and changing workforce patterns.[78] Both modifications modelled by GAO generally resulted in higher pension benefits, and address issues that may be of particular concern to women. In particular, in DC plans,[79] contributing early and maintaining an account over time has a significant positive impact on the balance of that account and the resulting retirement benefit. Decreasing vesting requirements would allow workers who change jobs more frequently to attain increased benefits from pension plans. Automatically rolling over accounts at a job's end increases the probability that accrued retirement balances will in fact be saved for retirement. The GEMINI/PENSIM models do not account for behavioural responses to program changes; therefore, data do not take into account possible employer or employee responses to the program modifications below.

Lowering Vesting Requirements

Under current law, eligible employees must be allowed to participate in a plan as of age 21 and after completing 1 year of service, subject to certain exceptions. An employee's own contributions to their pension plan are nonforfeitable, as are employer contributions once an employee's benefits have vested. ERISA, as amended, requires cliff vesting[80] in DBs within 5 years and full vesting under a graduated vesting[81] schedule within 7 years. cash balance plans ("hybrid" plans) generally will require vesting within 3 years. Beginning in 2008 employer contributions to DC plans[82] must vest in either a 3-year cliff or 6-year phased schedule (includes service prior to 2007).[83]

GAO Simulation of Lowered Vesting Requirements for Employer-Provided Pensions

Using the PENSIM microsimulation model, we projected the impact of a reduced vesting schedule on retirement benefits. For DB plans we specified 2- year cliff vesting, and for DC plans we specified 2-year cliff, and 3-year graduated vesting schedules. For the 1985 cohort, the median percentage change in benefit levels for women who were affected by the change was an increase of 6.29 percent. Similarly, men's median percentage change in benefits for those affected was of 5.74 percent.[84] (See table 11.) While the number of women affected by this change was fairly evenly distributed across the top four income quintiles with fewer in the lowest, the median percentage change in benefits is much larger for the women in the lowest quintile than in higher quintiles; for those in the lowest quintile, the median percentage change in benefit levels was more than four times the change for women in the highest quintile and nearly twice that of women in the second lowest income quintile. This suggests that increases in pension benefits gained as a result of this change represent a larger portion of total pension accumulation for less affluent women. Similarly, while the number of married women affected was larger than the number affected in other marital classifications, the median percentage change in benefits for never married and divorced women was almost twice the median percentage change in benefits for married and widowed women.

Table 11. Median Percentage Change in Pension Benefits for Individuals Born in 1985 Whose Benefits Changed After Lowered Vesting Schedules

<table>
<tr><td colspan="5">Numbers in percent</td></tr>
<tr><td colspan="3">All men</td><td colspan="2">All women</td></tr>
<tr><td colspan="3">5.74</td><td colspan="2">6.29</td></tr>
<tr><td colspan="5">Women by income quintile</td></tr>
<tr><td>Lowest quintile</td><td>Quintile 2</td><td>Middle quintile</td><td>Quintile 4</td><td>Highestquintile</td></tr>
<tr><td>16.37</td><td>8.90</td><td>6.18</td><td>5.11</td><td>3.51</td></tr>
<tr><td colspan="5">Women by marital status</td></tr>
<tr><td colspan="2">Never married</td><td>Divorced</td><td>Married</td><td>Widowed</td></tr>
<tr><td colspan="2">11.14</td><td>11.30</td><td>5.35</td><td>6.81</td></tr>
</table>

Source: GAO analysis based on the PENSIM model.
Note: Simulations calculated benefits for individuals at age 70 and were based on benefits adjusted for household size (for more information, see discussion of Family Equivalence Scale in appendix I). Income quintiles are based on the distribution of the present value of family lifetime earnings for the whole population (male and female). For percentage of population affected and results using the "Funded benefits" benchmark, see appendix II.

Table 12. Percentage of Total Simulation Population Whose Benefits Changed after Implementation of Lowered Vesting Schedules

Numbers in percent	
	Birth Cohort
	1985
All men	14.34
All women	12.62

Source: GAO analysis based on the GEMINI model.
Note: Simulations calculated benefits for individuals at age 70 and were based on benefits adjusted for household size (for more information, see discussion of Family Equivalence Scale in appendix I).

AUTOMATIC ROLLOVER UPON LEAVING EMPLOYMENT PRIOR TO RETIREMENT AGE

"Automatic rollover" proposals would maintain the level of accrued retirement benefits in DC plans when an individual switches jobs before retirement by automatically contributing retirement balances to a qualified retirement savings account. According to research conducted by the Employee Benefit Research Institute in 2003, under 50 percent of recipients of lump sum distributions between the ages of 30 and 50 reported using the entire portion for reinvestment into a qualified account.[85] For those aged 21 to 30, the percentage using the entire distribution for tax-qualified financial savings drops to under 35. This modification would provide greater retirement income for men and women. However, some research shows that women roll over a lower percentage of their accrued balances than men do;, because of this, requiring automatic rollover may have a larger effect on women overall.

GAO Simulation of 100 Percent Automatic Rollover for Employer- Provided Pensions

GAO used the GEMINI microsimulation model to determine what the impact could be on retirement benefit levels if 100 percent of accrued retirement balances were reinvested into qualified accounts after every job change until retirement. For the 1985 cohort, the median percentage change in benefits for those affected was quite similar for men and women, 7.3 percent and 7.63 percent, respectively. (See table 13.) This assumes that those affected would not make any changes in their savings or spending behavior to offset the requirement. Among women who were affected by the change, those who were never married or who were divorced had the largest percentage median increases in benefits. Additionally, while the number of women affected by this change again was fairly evenly distributed across the top four income quintiles with fewer in the lowest, those in the lowest two income quintiles had substantially larger median percentage changes in benefits than those in the highest two quintiles.

Table 13. Median Percentage Change in Pension Benefits for Individuals Born in 1985 Whose Benefits Changed after Implementation of 100 Percent Automatic Rollover

Numbers in percent				
All men		All women		
7.30		7.63		
Women by income quintile				
Lowest quintile	Quintile 2	Middle quintile	Quintile 4	Highestquintile
16.94	11.85	8.50	5.97	3.62
Women by marital status				
Never married	Divorced	Married	Widowed	
15.04	12.09	6.74	7.48	

Source: GAO analysis based on the PENSIM model.

Note: Simulations calculated benefits for individuals at age 70 and were based on benefits adjusted for household size (for more information, see discussion of Family Equivalence Scale in appendix I). Income quintiles are based on the distribution of the present value of family lifetime earnings for the whole population (male and female). For percentage of population affected and results using the "Funded benefits" benchmark, see appendix II.

Table 14. Percentage of Total Simulation Population Whose Benefits Changed after Implementation of 100 Percent Automatic Rollover

Numbers in percent	
	Birth Cohort
	1985
All men	12.26
All women	11.21

Source: GAO analysis based on the GEMINI model.

Note: Simulations calculated benefits for individuals at age 70 and were based on benefits adjusted for household size (for more information, see discussion of Family Equivalence Scale in appendix I).

Concluding Observations

Despite the increases in women's labor force participation over the past 55 years, certain groups of women will continue to be vulnerable to economic insecurity in retirement. While women are working more than in the past, they remain the primary source of family caregiving and are more likely than men either to reduce their workforce participation or never to enter the paid workforce. Consequently, despite elements of the Social Security and employer-sponsored pension systems that provide retirement income for low- or non-earning spouses, the remaining gaps between women's and men's labor force participation, earnings, and pension participation will continue to leave many women with fewer financial resources in retirement than men. In addition to the choices many women make to stay out of the workforce or to reduce the amount of their work, certain life events (such as divorce and widowhood) are likely to exacerbate this disparity. Ultimately, women's roles in the workplace and within a family may hinder them from building sufficient retirement resources, leaving them at greater risk of poverty in old age.

Other trends can exacerbate the vulnerability of women in retirement. Many proposed reforms for Social Security and employer-provided pensions have focused on long-term solvency and financing issues. Research has shown that many of these types of reforms have the potential to reduce retirement income from levels scheduled in current law for a large number of beneficiaries. This is of particular concern for women because of their reliance on Social Security as a main source of retirement income. Changes in the structure of employer-sponsored pensions, which can have some benefits for women, may also have some negative consequences. Although the shift to DC type plans can have a positive impact on people who change jobs frequently or work intermittently, such plans can transfer more of the responsibility to make prudent investment decisions and to manage longevity risk to individuals. While this is true for both men and women, it is of particular concern for women because of their greater longevity. Moreover, the original design of the Social Security system was based on a particular household structure—single earner families—and that structure is no longer the norm in America. If policy makers wish to design a system that adequately and equitably compensates all retirees, then it will be necessary to design a system that reflects the diversity of employment patterns and family structure within the population it serves. In fact, several past reform proposals included modernization elements that would target benefit enhancements to various subgroups.

In contemplating modifications to Social Security or employer-provided pensions, it is helpful to understand all possible effects, including the impact on Social Security solvency or costs to employers. Each of the Social Security changes that we modeled would have small, but negative, effects on program solvency. Small effects such as these, when included in a larger package of reforms, could be overwhelmed by the effects of other changes. Nevertheless, the trade-offs between enhanced benefits and costs are always important to consider. It is also helpful to understand how changes may affect different types of individuals with different work and earnings histories—for example, women who never enter the workforce or choose to reduce their work, possibly to care for children or other family members. Changes to benefit structures may also have different effects on individuals within different family structures, such as singleearner married couples, dual-earner households, or unmarried heads of household. Recognizing these differences is important not only in terms of improving adequacy and equity in the benefit structure, but also in understanding how different benefit structures might affect the choices individuals make regarding their own workforce attachment. With such knowledge, policy makers have the potential to mitigate both existing disparities in retirement income as well as the differential effects of reforms.

AGENCY COMMENTS

We provided a draft of this report to the departments of Labor and the Treasury, the Internal Revenue Service, and the Social Security Administration. The departments of Labor and the Treasury and the Social Security Administration provided technical comments, which we incorporated where appropriate.

We are sending copies of this report to the Secretary of Labor, the Commissioner of Internal Revenue, the Commissioner of Social Security, the Secretary of the Treasury, and appropriate congressional committees, and other interested parties. We will also make copies available to others upon request. In addition, the report will be available at no charge on GAO's Web site at http://www.gao.gov.

If you or your staff have any questions about this report, please contact me at (202) 512-7215 or at bovbjergb@gao.gov. Contact points for our Offices of Congressional Relations and Public Affairs may be found on the last page of this report. GAO staff who made major contributions to this report are listed in appendix V.

Barbara D. Bovbjerg, Director
Education, Workforce, and
Income Security Issues

APPENDIX I: METHODOLOGY

To identify the effects of individual reform elements on Social Security and pension benefit levels for women, we used the Policy Simulation Group's (PSG) microsimulation models to simulate Social Security benefits and pension income.

For our simulations, we used PSG's Social Security and Accounts Simulator (SSASIM), Genuine Microsimulation of Social Security Accounts (GEMINI), and Pension Simulator (PENSIM) simulation models. GEMINI simulates Social Security benefits and taxes for large representative samples of people born in the same year. GEMINI simulates all types of Social Security benefits including retired workers', spouses', survivors', and disability benefits. It can be used to model a variety of changes to Social Security. GEMINI uses inputs from SSASIM, which has been used in numerous GAO reports, and PENSIM, which was developed for the Department of Labor. GEMINI relies on SSASIM for economic and demographic projections and relies on PENSIM for simulated life histories of large representative samples of people born in the same year and their spouses.[86] Life histories include educational attainment, labor force participation, earnings, job mobility, marriage, disability, childbirth, retirement, and death. Life histories are validated against data from the Survey of Income and Program Participation, the Current Population Survey, Modeling

Income in the Near Term (MINT3),[87] and the Panel Study of Income Dynamics. Additionally, any projected statistics (such as life expectancy, employment patterns, and marital status at age 60) are, where possible, consistent with intermediate cost projections from the Social Security Administration's Office of the Chief Actuary (OCACT). At their best, such models can provide only very rough estimates of future incomes. However, these estimates may be useful for comparing future incomes across alternative policy scenarios and over time.

GEMINI can be operated as a free-standing model or it can operate as a SSASIM add-on. When operating as an add-on, GEMINI is started automatically by SSASIM for one of two purposes. GEMINI can enable the SSASIM macro model to operate in the Overlapping Cohorts (OLC) mode or it can enable the SSASIM micro model to operate in the Representative Cohort Sample (RCS) mode. The SSASIM OLC mode requests GEMINI to produce samples for each cohort born after 1934 in order to build up aggregate payroll tax revenues and (Old-Age, Survivors, and Disability Insurance) OASDI benefit expenditures for each calendar year, which are used by SSASIM to calculate standard trust fund financial statistics. In either mode, GEMINI operates with the same logic, but typically with smaller cohort sample sizes in OLC mode than in the RCS or stand-alonemodel mode.

Using the GEMINI model, we estimated Social Security benefits at age 70 for approximately 2 percent of individuals born in each of two illustrative birth cohorts, 1950 (resulting in a sample of 63,813 individuals) and 1985 (resulting in a sample of 78,857 individuals). We also used the PENSIM model to estimate pension income for those born in 1985.[88] We simulated Social Security benefits for two cohorts in order to identify differences in the effects of modifications that could be due to variations in labor force participation across generations. We also used the microsimulation models to simulate Social Security benefits, pension income, and the earnings of spouses not yet retired, in order to explore the relationships between benefit levels and workforce attachment and marital status. For this analysis we simulated benefit levels at ages 67 and 85 for the 1985 birth cohort. These models do not include measures of personal savings, earnings in retirement, health benefits, or income from other income support programs.

Additionally, we evaluated the effect of Social Security modifications on a "low benefit avoidance rate," a measure produced by the model that proxies for poverty avoidance. However, it does not include pension income or savings, and so cannot be called a poverty avoidance measure. The low benefit avoidance rate is expressed as the percentage of retirement years in which an individual's Social Security benefits (plus any earnings) are above a low-benefit threshold in the GEMINI model (the thresholds are $9,669 for individuals and $12,186 for couples, in 2007 dollars). Both income and the threshold are based on individual data when unmarried and on couple data when married. Benefits and taxes were simulated under our tax increase only (promised benefits) and proportional benefit reduction (funded benefits) benchmarks (described below) and certain specific individual programmatic changes. These simulations are based on the Social Security Trustees' 2007 intermediate economic and actuarial assumptions. While our simulations provide projections of future retirement income, there is a considerable amount of uncertainty involved with these estimates. Since these estimates could change significantly, depending on assumptions used and behavior responses, they should not be considered predictions. Furthermore, because simulations are sensitive to economic and demographic assumptions, it is generally more appropriate to compare benefits across the scenarios than to focus on the actual estimates themselves. Therefore, to avoid inappropriate comparisons, we evaluated the effects of modifications based on the changes in benefit levels rather than comparing actual benefit levels.

In general, GAO has suggested that policy makers should consider three basic criteria when evaluating reform proposals[89]

- the extent to which the proposal achieves sustainable solvency and how the proposal would affect the economy and the federal budget;
- the balance struck between the goals of individual equity[90] (rates of return on individual contributions) and income adequacy[91] (level and certainty of monthly benefits); and
- how readily such changes could be implemented, administered, and explained to the public.

Moreover, changes to the system should be evaluated as packages that strike a balance among the individual elements of the proposal and the interactions among these elements. The overall evaluation of any particular reform proposal depends on the weight individual policy makers place on each of the above criteria.

However, for the purposes of this study we evaluated only specific individual modifications. We looked at certain specific changes in order to focus on those that account for more recent shifts in family structure and labor force composition. In particular, we wanted to identify the direction of the impact of modifications that might be used to mitigate the effects of broad reform packages likely to reduce benefits. Nevertheless, we recognize that there could be important interaction effects with any set of reforms and maintain the importance of considering all possible effects of any reform package as a whole. The solvency impact of any single programmatic change may be marginal and, as part of a package, could be overwhelmed by other changes. Nevertheless, in appendix IV, we have provided the impact of each change on the Social Security Trust Fund balance, after achieving 75-year solvency with the benchmark scenarios. Additionally, because we simulated programmatic changes in isolation we could not calculate traditional equity measures, which relate benefits received to taxes paid. Because we simulated programmatic changes in isolation on top of solvent benchmark scenarios, the results did not achieve long-term solvency. We did not speculate on how the changes would be paid for in the context of overall reform. Without information on total contributions or benefits under each simulation, traditional equity measures would not be meaningful. Finally, given the limited scope of the changes we simulated, we did not address issues of implementation, administration, or public comprehension.

Assumptions and Limitations

Simulating retirement income almost 50 years into the future requires many assumptions and simplifications, and consequently, our simulations have a number of limitations. A primary limitation of our analysis is that it does not include important components of retirement income such as personal savings, earnings in retirement, health benefits, and other public assistance programs such as Supplemental Security Income (SSI). To facilitate our modeling analysis, we made a variety of assumptions regarding economic and demographic trends. In choosing our assumptions, we focused our analysis to illustrate relevant points about distributional effects and hold equal as much as possible any variables that were either not relevant to or would unduly complicate that focus. As a result of these assumptions, as well as issues inherent in any modelling effort, our analysis has some key limitations.

2007 Social Security Trustees' Assumptions

The simulations are based on economic and demographic assumptions from the 2007 Social Security Trustees' report.[92] We used the Trustees' intermediate assumptions for inflation, real wage growth, mortality decline, immigration, labor force participation, and interest rates.

Family Equivalence Scale

For some of our analyses, we used a measure of income adjusted to account for household size and economies of scale. We did this to facilitate comparisons between nonmarried persons and married persons whose household income includes income from both spouses that can vary significantly between them. For instance, although a married couple may need approximately twice as much for food and clothing as a single person, other needs, such as housing and transportation, are not additive in the same way. However, the effect of using data adjusted for household size on a reform targeted at married couples, such as a change in spousal benefits, is that the change in benefits resulting from the program modification is shared by both the husband and the wife. Thus, population data based on the adjusted measure describe the number of people whose household had a benefit change resulting from the modification. For example, in the "Decreased Spousal Benefit and Increased Survivor Benefit" modification, the family equivalence data indicate that a nearly equal percent of men and women are affected by the modification because the effect of the benefit change is shared by both spouses. Therefore, in order to identify just the percent of men and women who had changes to their own benefit as a result of the program change, percentages are also calculated based on benefits not adjusted for household size.

The adjustment is made by dividing household benefit levels by a "family equivalence scale."[93] This equivalence scale reflects both differences in consumption by adults and children under 18 and the economies of scale that benefit families. The family equivalence scale in the GEMINI model (shown below) and its default parameters are based on the recommendations of the National Academy of Sciences' Panel on Poverty and Family Assistance.

$$\text{Family equivalence scale} = (A + P*k)^f$$

where A is the number of adults in the family, k is the number of children, each of whom is treated as a proportion P of an adult, and f is the scale economy factor.

Thus, the formula calculates the number of adult equivalents (A + P*k) and raises the result to a power f that reflects economies of scale for families. We used the default parameters in the model, so that both P and f are 0.70.

Description of Simulated Social Security Modifications

Dependent Care Credit—Analyzing Impact of Inserting a "Credit"

To simulate a dependent care credit we provided a "credit" in the OASDI work record that would top off a year's earnings to the level of half of average wages. In a given year, the OASDI work records of individuals with a child 5 years of age or under and who had earnings less than onehalf of average wages were credited with one half of average wages (as measured by the Average Wage Index used by the Social Security Administration). A lifetime maximum of five credits was allowed. If both parents met these criteria in any given year, only the lower-earning parent received the credit; if both parent's earnings were identical in any given year, the credit was split evenly. Credits were not counted toward benefit eligibility. In our simulation the reform went into effect in 2010. This change as specified has not been scored publicly by OCACT. Using the OLC mode of SSASIM that mimics the intermediate assumptions of the 2007 Trustees' report, we estimated this modification as increasing the size of the long-range actuarial deficit by 0.19 percent under the "promised benefits" benchmark and by 0.17 under the "funded benefits" benchmark.

Decrease Spousal Benefit/Increase Survivor Benefit

To simulate the effects of a decrease in spousal benefits paired with an increase in survivor benefits, we reduced spousal benefits from one-half to one-third of the retired worker's benefit. We also increased the survivor benefit to 75 percent of the couple's previous combined benefit level, if higher than the survivor benefit available under current law. The benefit of this reform is capped at the average PIA for all new retirees. Our simulation of the reform went into effect in 2010.

These changes as specified have not been scored publicly by OCACT.[94] Using the OLC mode of SSASIM that mimics the intermediate assumptions of the 2007 Trustees' report, we estimated this modification as decreasing the size of the long-range actuarial deficit by 0.02 percent under the "promised benefits" benchmark and increasing the size of the long range actuarial deficit by 0.06 under the "funded benefits" benchmark.

Increased Survivor Benefit Only

We also simulated the effects of an increase in survivor benefits independently. To do this, as above, we increased the survivor benefit to 75 percent of the couple's previous combined benefit level, if higher than the survivor benefit available under current law. The benefit of this reform is capped at the average PIA for all new retirees. Our simulation of the reform went into effect in 2010.

This change is similar to one scored by OCACT as part of the *OASDI Financial Effects of the Social Security Guarantee Plus Act of 2005 (May 12, 2005),* which estimated a 0.08 percent increase to the long-range actuarial deficit, and *Estimated OASDI Financial Effects of the Bipartisan Retirement Security Act of 2005 (November 4, 2005),* which also estimated a 0.08 percent increase to the long-range actuarial. Using the OLC mode of SSASIM that mimics the intermediate assumptions of the 2007 Trustees' report, we estimated this modification as increasing the size of the long-range actuarial deficit by 0.07 percent under the "promised benefits" benchmark and by 0.14 percent under the "funded benefits" benchmark.

Reduce 10-Year Marriage Requirement

To simulate the effects of a reduced marriage requirement to qualify for divorced spouse benefits, we reduced duration of marriage requirements from 10 to 7 years. In our simulation, this reform took effect in 2010. This change as specified has not been scored publicly by OCACT. Using the OLC mode of SSASIM that mimics the intermediate assumptions of the 2007 Trustees' report, we estimated this change as increasing the size of the long-range actuarial deficit by 0.02 percent under the "promised benefits" benchmark and increasing the size of the long-range actuarial deficit by 0.06 under the "funded benefits" benchmark.

Increase/Strengthen Minimum Benefit

To simulate an increased minimum benefit, we provided a partial benefit enhancement for workers with more than 80 quarters of coverage and provide a full benefit enhancement to workers with 120 quarters of coverage. It would equal 120 percent of the aged poverty threshold for workers with 120 quarters of coverage and be linearly prorated to zero for workers with 80 quarters of coverage. These provisions would also apply in determining the PIA levels used for calculating auxiliary benefits and DI benefits. The first year of full implementation is 2010.

This modification as specified has not been scored publicly by OCACT. Using the OLC mode of SSASIM that mimics the intermediate assumptions of the 2007 Trustees' report, we estimated this change as increasing the size of the long-range actuarial deficit by 0.05 percent under the "promised benefits" benchmark and increasing the size of the long range actuarial deficit by 0.13 percent under the "funded benefits" benchmark as well.

Description of Simulated Pension Modifications

Decrease Vesting Requirements

In our modeling of this modification, we reduced maximum allowable vesting periods to 2 years for all pension programs with cliff vesting and 3 years for all pension programs with graduated vesting. If plans within the model already used shorter vesting schedules, those vesting schedules remained unchanged. In our simulation, this change took effect in 2010.

Automatic Rollover

In order to consider the potential upper bound of impact for a modification that would ensure full rollover of retirement assets at preretirement job terminations, we modeled a full rollover of retirement balances into qualified accounts. In our simulation, this change took effect in 2010.

Data Reliability

To assess the reliability of simulated data from GEMINI, we reviewed PSG's published validation checks, examined the data for reasonableness and consistency, and compared our solvency estimates, where applicable, with published results from the actuaries at the Social Security Administration.

PSG has published a number of validation checks of its simulated life histories. For example, simulated life expectancy is compared with projections from the Social Security Trustees; simulated benefits at age 62 are compared with administrative data from SSA; and simulated educational attainment, labor force participation rates, and job tenure are compared with values from the Current Population Survey. We found that simulated statistics for the life histories were reasonably close to the validation targets.

Benchmark Policy Scenarios

According to current projections of the Social Security Trustees for the next 75 years, revenues will not be adequate to pay full benefits as defined by the current benefit formula. Therefore, estimating future Social Security benefits should reflect that actuarial deficit and account for the fact that some combination of benefit reductions and revenue increases will be necessary to restore long-term solvency.

To illustrate a full range of possible outcomes, we developed hypothetical benchmark policy scenarios that would achieve 75-year solvency either by only increasing payroll taxes or by only reducing benefits.[95] In developing these benchmarks, we identified criteria to use to guide their design and selection. Our tax-increase-only benchmark simulates "promised benefits," or those benefits promised by the current benefit formula, while our benefit-reduction-only benchmark simulates "funded benefits," or those benefits for which currently scheduled revenues are projected to be sufficient. Under the latter policy scenario, the benefit reductions would be phased in between 2010 and 2040 to strike a balance between the size of the incremental reductions each year and the size of the ultimate reduction.

Social Security Administration (SSA) actuaries scored our original 2001 benchmark policies and determined the parameters for each that would achieve 75-year solvency.[96] Table 8 summarizes our benchmark policy scenarios. For our benefit reduction scenario, the actuaries determined these parameters assuming that disabled and survivor benefits would be reduced on the same basis as retired worker and dependent benefits. If disabled and survivor benefits were not reduced at all, reductions in other benefits would be greater than shown in this analysis.

Table 15. Summary of Benchmark Policy Scenarios

Benchmark policy scenario	Description	Phase-in period	Ultimate new benefit reductions[a] (percent)
Tax increase only (promised benefits)	Increases payroll taxes in 2008by amount necessary to achieve 75-year solvency (0.98percent of payroll each for employees and employers)	Immediate	0
Proportional benefit reduction (funded benefits)	Reduces benefit formula factors proportionally across all earnings levels	2013-2043	27

Source: GAO.

[a] These benefit reduction amounts do not reflect the implicit reductions resulting from the gradual increase in the full retirement age that has already been enacted.

Criteria

According to our analysis, appropriate benchmark policies should ideally be evaluated against the following criteria:

1. *Distributional neutrality:* The benchmark should reflect the current system as closely as possible while still restoring solvency. In particular, it should try to reflect the goals and effects of the current system with respect to redistribution of income. However, there are many possible ways to interpret what this means, such as

a. producing a distribution of benefit levels with a shape similar to the distribution under the current benefit formula (as measured by coefficients of variation, skewness, kurtosis, and so forth);
b. maintaining a proportional level of income transfers in dollars;
c. maintaining proportional replacement rates; and
d. maintaining proportional rates of return.

2. Demarcating upper and lower bounds: These would be the bounds within which the effects of alternative proposals would fall. For example, one benchmark would reflect

restoring solvency solely by increasing payroll taxes and therefore maximizing benefit levels, while another would solely reduce benefits and therefore minimize payroll tax rates.

3. Ability to model: The benchmark should lend itself to being modelled within the GEMINI model.

4. Plausibility: The benchmark should serve as a reasonable alternative within the current debate; otherwise, the benchmark could be perceived as an invalid basis for comparison.

5. Transparency: The benchmark should be readily explainable to the reader.

Tax-Increase-Only or "Promised Benefits," Benchmark Policies

Our tax-increase-only benchmark would raise payroll taxes once and immediately by the amount of Social Security's actuarial deficit as a percentage of payroll. It results in the smallest ultimate tax rate of those we considered and spreads the tax burden most evenly across generations; this is the primary basis for our selection. The later that taxes are increased, the higher the ultimate tax rate needed to achieve solvency, and in turn the higher the tax burden on later taxpayers and lower on earlier taxpayers. Still, any policy scenario that achieves 75-year solvency only by increasing revenues would have the same effect on the adequacy of future benefits in that promised benefits would not be reduced. Nevertheless, alternative approaches to increasing revenues could have very different effects on individual equity.

Benefit-Reduction-Only, or "Funded Benefits," Benchmark Policies

We developed alternative benefit reduction benchmarks for our analysis. For ease of modeling, all benefit reduction benchmarks take the form of reductions in the benefit formula factors; they differ in the relative size of those reductions across the three factors, which are 90, 32, and 15 percent under the current formula. Each benchmark has three dimensions of specification: scope, phase-in period, and the factor changes themselves. For our analysis, we apply benefit reductions in our benchmarks very generally to all types of benefits, including disability and survivors' benefits as well as old-age benefits. Our objective is to find policies that achieve solvency while reflecting the distributional effects of the current program as closely as possible. Therefore, it would not be appropriate to reduce some benefits and not others. If disabled and survivor benefits were not reduced at all, reductions in other benefits would be deeper than shown in this analysis.

Phase-in Period

We selected a phase-in period that begins with those becoming initially entitled in 2013 and continues for 30 years. We chose this phase-in period to achieve a balance between two competing objectives: (1) minimizing the size of the ultimate benefit reduction and (2) minimizing the size of each year's incremental reduction to avoid "notches," or unduly large incremental reductions. Notches create marked inequities between beneficiaries close in age to each other. Later birth cohorts are generally agreed to experience lower rates of return on their contributions already under the current system. Therefore, minimizing the size of the ultimate benefit reduction would also minimize further reductions in rates of return for later cohorts. The smaller each year's reduction, the longer it will take for benefit reductions to achieve solvency, and in turn the greater the eventual reductions will have to be. However, the smallest possible ultimate reduction would be achieved by reducing benefits immediately for all new retirees by 13 percent; this would create a notch.

In addition, we feel it is appropriate to delay the first year of the benefit reductions for a few years because those within a few years of retirement would not have adequate time to adjust their retirement planning if the reductions applied immediately. The Maintain Tax Rates (MTR) benchmark in the 1994-1996 Advisory Council report also provided for a similar delay.[97]

Finally, the timing of any policy changes in a benchmark scenario should be consistent with the proposals against which the benchmark is compared. The analysis of any proposal assumes that the proposal is enacted, usually within a few years. Consistency requires that any benchmark also assumes enactment of the benchmark policy in the same time frame. Some analysts have suggested using a benchmark scenario in which Congress does not act at all and the trust funds become exhausted.[98]

However, such a benchmark assumes that no action is taken, while the proposals against which it is compared assume that action is taken, which is inconsistent. It also seems unlikely that a policy enacted over the next few years would wait to reduce benefits until the trust funds are exhausted; such a policy would result in a sudden large benefit reduction and create substantial inequities across generations.

Defining the PIA Formula Factor Reductions

When workers retire, become disabled, or die, Social Security uses their lifetime earnings records to determine each worker's PIA, on which the initial benefit and auxiliary benefits are based. The PIA is the result of two elements—the Average Indexed Monthly Earnings (AIME) and the benefit formula. The AIME is determined by taking the lifetime earnings record, indexing it, and taking the average of the highest 35 years of indexed wages.[99] To determine the PIA, the AIME is then applied to a step-like formula, shown here for 2007.

$$
\begin{aligned}
PIA = {} & 90\% \, (AIME_1 \leq \$680) \\
& + 32\% \, (AIME_2 > \$680 \text{ and } \leq \$4100) \\
& + 15\% \, (AIME_3 > \$4100)
\end{aligned}
$$

where AIMEi is the applicable portion of AIME.

All of our benefit-reduction benchmarks are variations of changes in PIA formula factors.

Proportional Reduction

Each formula factor is reduced annually by subtracting a constant proportion of that factor's value under current law, resulting in a constant percentage reduction of currently promised benefits for everyone. That is,

$$F^{1}_{t+1} = F^{1}_{t} - (F^{1}_{2008} \bullet x)$$

where F_t^i represents the three PIA formula factors in year t and x = constant proportional formula factor reduction.

The value of x is calculated to achieve 75-year solvency, given the chosen phase-in period and scope of reductions.

The formula for this reduction specifies that the proportional reduction is always taken as a proportion of the current law factors rather than the factors for each preceding year. This maintains a constant rate of benefit reduction from year to year. In contrast, taking the reduction as a proportion of each preceding year's factors implies a decelerating of the benefit reduction over time because each preceding year's factors get smaller with each reduction. To achieve the same level of 75-year solvency, this would require a greater proportional reduction in earlier years because of the smaller reductions in later years.

The proportional reduction hits lower earners harder than higher earners because the constant x percent of the higher formula factors results in a larger percentage reduction over the lower earnings segments of the formula. For example, in a year when the cumulative size of the proportional reduction has reached 10 percent, the 90 percent factor would then have been reduced by 9 percentage points, the 32 percent factor by 3.2 percentage points, and the 15 percent factor by 1.5 percentage points. As a result, earnings in the first segment of the benefit formula would be replaced at 9 percentage points less than the current formula, while earnings in the third segment of the formula would be replaced at only 1.5 percentage points less than the current formula.[100] Table 9 summarizes the features of our benchmarks.

Table 16. Summary of Benchmark Policy Scenario Parameters

		Annual PIA factor reduction (percentage point)			Ultimate PIA factor (2043) (percent)		
Benchmark policy scenario	Phase-in period	90 percent factor	32 percent factor	15 percent factor	90 percent factor	32 percent factor	15 percent factor
Tax increase only (promised benefits)	2008	0	0	0	90.00	32.00	15.00
Proportional benefit reduction (funded benefits)	2013-2043	0.80	0.28	0.13	65.28	23.21	10.88

Source: GAO's analysis as scored by SSA actuaries.

Note: Annual PIA factor reductions rounded to the nearest hundredth of a percent.

Appendix II: Simulation Results for Social Security Modifications

To account for differences in household size and economies of scale associated with larger households, we based our analyses on benefit levels adjusted for household size (see app. I for more information). However, the effect of using data adjusted for household size on a reform targeted at married couples, such as a change in spousal benefits, is that the change in benefits resulting from the program modification is shared by both the husband and the wife. Thus, population data based on the adjusted measure describe the number of people whose household had a benefit change resulting from the modification. For example, in the

"Decreased Spousal Benefit and Increased Survivor Benefit" modification, the family equivalence data indicate that a nearly equal percent of men and women are affected by the modification because the effect of the benefit change is shared by both spouses. Therefore, in order to identify only the percent of men and women who had changes to their own benefit as a result of the program change, percentages are also calculated based on benefits not adjusted for household size.

Table 17. Simulation Results of the Dependent Care Credit under Alternative Benchmark Scenarios, for the 1950 and 1985 Birth Cohorts

Dependent care credit				
Benchmark	Cohort		All men	All women
	Percentage change in median benefitsfor individualswhose benefitschanged, benefitsadjusted for household size			
Promised benefits	1950		2.60	3.24
	1985	2.06	2.63	
Funded benefits	1950		2.58	3.24
	1985	2.07	2.61	
	Percentage of specified subpopulation of simulated sample whose benefitschanged, benefitsadjusted for household size			
Promised benefits	1950		60.71	57.98
	1985	57.05	60.52	
Funded benefits	1950		60.47	58.04
	1985	56.94	60.25	
	Percentage of total simulation population whose benefitschanged, benefitsadjusted for household size			
Promised benefits	1950		28.43	30.83
	1985	35.06	30.99	
Funded benefits	1950		28.32	30.86
	1985	27.79	30.84	
	Percentage of specified subpopulation of simulated sample whose benefitschanged, individual benefitsnot adjusted for household size			
Promised benefits	1950		47.85	52.56
	1985	44.21	55.59	
Funded benefits	1950		47.83	52.60
	1985	44.13	55.27	
	Percentage of total simulation population whose benefitschanged, individual benefitsnot adjusted for household size			

Dependent care credit				
Benchmark	Cohort		All men	All women
Promised benefits	1950		22.11	28.27
	1985	21.38	8.71	
Funded benefits	1950		22.11	28.29
	1985	21.34	28.54	

Source: GAO analysis of GEMINI model.

Note: Simulations calculated benefits for individuals at age 70.

Table 18. Simulation Results for Dependent Care Credit by Income Quintile under Alternative Benchmark Scenarios, for the 1950 and 1985 Birth Cohorts

Women only							
Benchmark	Cohort	Lowest quintile		Quintile 2	Middle quintile	Quintile 4	Highest quintile
	Percentage change in median benefitsfor individualswhose benefitschanged, benefitsadjusted for household size						
Promised benefits	1950	7.96		4.16	2.80	1.68	0.92
	1985	6.88	3.50	2.12	1.14	0.72	
Funded benefits	1950	7.96		4.16	2.82	1.68	0.93
	1985	6.85	3.51	2.10	1.13	0.72	
	Percentage of women in each income quintile whose benefitschanged, benefitsadjusted for household size						
Promised benefits	1950	65.03		64.71	59.36	52.63	43.16
	1985	73.41	68.15	58.93	54.00	43.31	
Funded benefits	1950	65.06		64.75	59.39	52.72	43.28
	1985	72.78	67.84	58.76	53.95	43.14	
	Percentage of total simulation population whose benefits changed, benefits adjusted for household size						
Promised benefits	1950	7.25		8.13	6.52	5.30	3.62
	1985	8.09	7.63	6.26	5.33	3.68	
Funded benefits	1950	7.25		8.14	6.53	5.31	3.63
	1985	8.02	7.59	6.24	5.32	3.66	

Source: GAO analysis of GEMINI model.

Note: Simulations calculated benefits for individuals at age 70. Income quintiles are based on the distribution of the present value of family lifetime earnings for the whole population (male and female).

Table 19. Simulation Results for Dependent Care Credit by Marital Status under Alternative Benchmark Scenarios, for the 1950 and 1985 Birth Cohorts

Women only					
Benchmark	Cohort	Never married	Divorced	Married	Widowed
	Percentage change in median benefitsfor women whose benefitschanged, benefitsadjusted for household size				
Promised benefits	1950	7.95	5.05	2.64	2.87
	1985	6.69	4.18	2.19	2.43
Funded benefits	1950	7.95	5.05	2.65	2.87
	1985	6.69	4.15	2.18	2.37
	Percentage of women in each marital statuswhose benefitschanged, benefitsadjusted for household size				
Promised benefits	1950	21.06	65.71	64.09	52.39
	1985	21.81	67.24	66.85	59.62
Women only					
Benchmark	Cohort	Never married	Divorced	Married	Widowed
Funded benefits	1950	21.06	65.75	64.21	52.39
	1985	21.81	67.08	66.61	58.85
	Percentage of total simulation population whose benefitschanged, benefitsadjusted for household size				
Promised benefits	1950	0.97	8.21	15.04	6.61
	1985	1.30	6.89	17.96	4.83
Funded benefits	1950	0.97	8.21	15.07	6.61
	1985	1.30	6.87	17.90	4.77

Source: GAO analysis of GEMINI model.

Note: Simulations calculated benefits for individuals at age 70.

Table 20. Simulation Results for Increased Survivor Benefit Only under Alternative Benchmark Scenarios, for the 1950 and 1985 Birth Cohorts

Increased survivor benefit only			
Benchmark	Cohort	All men	All women
	Percentage change in median benefitsfor individualswhose benefits changed, benefits adjusted for household size		
Promised benefits	1950	28.78	15.71
	1985	28.98	18.36
Funded benefits	1950	28.36	15.71
	1985	28.57	20.09
	Percentage of specified subpopulation of simulated sample whose benefits changed, benefits adjusted for household size		
Promised benefits	1950	1.66	3.97
	1985	0.95	2.20
Funded benefits	1950	1.67	3.97
	1985	1.76	3.96
	Percentage of total simulation population whose benefitschanged, benefits adjusted for household size		
Promised benefits	1950	0.78	2.11
	1985	0.46	1.13
Funded benefits	1950	0.78	2.11
	1985	0.86	2.03
	Percentage of specified subpopulation of simulated sample whose benefits changed, individual benefits not adjusted for household size		
Promised benefits	1950	1.59	3.71
	1985	0.93	2.10
Funded benefits	1950	1.60	3.71
	1985	1.71	3.79
	Percentage of total simulation population whose benefits changed, individual benefits not adjusted for household size		
Promised benefits	1950	0.74	2.00
	1985	0.45	1.09
Funded benefits	1950	0.74	2.00
	1985	0.83	1.96

Source: GAO analysis of GEMINI model.

Note: Simulations calculated benefits for individuals at age 70.

Table 21. Simulation Results for Increased Survivor Benefit Only by Income Quintile under Alternative Benchmark Scenarios, for the 1950 and 1985 Birth Cohorts

	Women only					
Benchmark	Cohort	Lowest quintile	Quintile 2	Middle quintile	Quintile 4	Highest quintile
	Percentage change in median benefits for individuals whose benefits changed, benefits adjusted for household size					
Promised benefits	1950	14.81	16.28	15.77	13.69	24.44
	1985	19.39	18.40	16.00	16.00	8.67
Funded benefits	1950	14.81	16.46	15.77	14.59	24.44
	1985	19.64	22.08	21.03	20.75	11.40
	Percentage of women in each income quintile whose benefits changed, benefits adjusted for household size					
Promised	1950	7.48	6.80	2.96	0.72	0.26

benefits	1985	5.02	3.51	1.33	0.31	0.09
Funded benefits	1950	7.48	6.80	2.96	0.72	0.26
	1985	5.63	5.88	4.09	2.49	0.84
	Percentage of total simulation population whose benefits changed, benefits adjusted for household size					
Promised benefits	1950	0.83	0.85	0.33	0.07	0.02
	1985	0.55	0.39	0.14	0.03	0.01
Funded benefits	1950	0.83	0.85	0.33	0.07	0.02
	1985	0.62	0.66	0.43	0.25	0.07

Source: GAO analysis of GEMINI model.

Note: Simulations calculated benefits for individuals at age 70. Income quintiles are based on the distribution of the present value of family lifetime earnings for the whole population (male and female).

Table 22. Simulation Results for Increased Survivor Benefit Only by Marital Status under Alternative Benchmark Scenarios, for the 1950 and 1985 Birth Cohorts

Women only					
Benchmark	Cohort	Never married	Divorced	Married	Widowed
	Percentage change in median benefitsfor women whose benefitschanged, benefitsadjusted for household size				
Promised benefits	1950	0	16.67	0	15.58
	1985	0	18.42	0	18.35
Funded benefits	1950	0	16.67	0	15.58
	1985	0	21.22	0	19.65
	Percentage of women in each marital statuswhose benefitschanged, benefitsadjusted for household size				
Promised benefits	1950	0	2.62	0	14.12
	1985	0	1.60	0	11.86
Funded benefits	1950	0	2.62	0	14.12
	1985	0	2.73	0	21.58
	Percentage of total simulation population whose benefitschanged, benefitsadjusted for household size				
Promised benefits	1950	0	0.33	0	1.78
	1985	0	0.16	0	0.96
Women only					
Benchmark	Cohort	Never married	Divorced	Married	Widowed
Funded benefits	1950	0	0.33	0	1.78
	1985	0	0.28	0	1.75

Source: GAO analysis of GEMINI model.

Note: Simulations calculated benefits for individuals at age 70.

Table 23. Simulation Results for Increased Survivor Benefit and Decreased Spouse Benefit under Alternative Benchmark Scenarios, for the 1950 and 1985 Birth Cohorts

	Increased survivor benefit and decreased spousal benefit		
Benchmark	Cohort	All men	All women
	Percentage change in median benefits for individuals whose benefits changed, benefits adjusted for household size		
Promised benefits	1950	-2.81	-2.66
	1985	-9.14	-8.78
Funded benefits	1950	-2.86	-2.66
	1985	-8.77	-7.98
	Percentage of specified subpopulation of simulated sample whose benefits changed, benefits adjusted for household size		
Promised benefits	1950	24.45	22.16
	1985	23.73	22.09
Funded benefits	1950	24.83	22.01
	1985	24.35	23.65
	Percentage of total simulation population whose benefits changed, benefits adjusted for household size		
Promised benefits	1950	11.45	11.78
	1985	11.58	11.31
Funded benefits	1950	11.63	11.70
	1985	11.89	12.11
	Percentage of specified subpopulation of simulated sample whose benefits changed, individual benefits not adjusted for household size		
Promised benefits	1950	4.82	19.28
	1985	5.22	16.81
Funded benefits	1950	4.71	19.10
	1985	5.83	18.57
	Percentage of total simulation population whose benefits changed, individual benefits not adjusted for household size		
Promised benefits	1950	2.23	10.37
	1985	2.53	8.68
Funded benefits	1950	2.18	10.27
	1985	2.82	9.59

Source: GAO analysis of GEMINI model.

Note: Simulations calculated benefits for individuals at age 70.

Table 24. Simulation Results for Increased Survivor Benefit and Decreased Spouse Benefit by Income Quintile under Alternative Benchmark Scenarios, for the 1950 and 1985 Birth Cohorts

	Women only					
Benchmark	Cohort	Lowest quintile	Quintile 2	Middle quintile	Quintile 4	Highest quintile
	Percentage change in median benefits for individuals whose benefits changed, benefits adjusted for household size					
Promised benefits	1950	-2.55	-2.55	-2.66	-2.67	-2.67
	1985	-9.82	-8.06	-8.21	-8.45	-9.27
Funded benefits	1950	-2.55	-2.54	-2.66	-2.67	-2.67
	1985	-9.52	-6.71	-6.99	-7.73	-9.09
	Percentage of women in each income quintile whose benefits changed, benefits adjusted for household size					
Promised benefits	1950	24.40	22.56	20.51	21.37	21.72
	1985	23.25	21.44	22.50	22.75	20.14

Funded benefits	1950	24.33	22.36	20.28	21.22	21.64
	1985	24.31	23.41	24.83	24.74	20.39
	Percentage of total simulation population whose benefits changed, benefits adjusted for household size					
Promised benefits	1950	2.72	2.84	2.25	2.15	1.82
	1985	2.56	2.40	2.39	2.24	1.71
Funded benefits	1950	2.71	2.81	2.23	2.14	1.81
	1985	2.68	2.62	2.64	2.44	1.73

Source: GAO analysis of GEMINI model.

Note: Simulations calculated benefits for individuals at age 70. Income quintiles are based on the distribution of the present value of family lifetime earnings for the whole population (male and female).

Table 25. Simulation Results for Increased Survivor Benefit and Decreased Spouse Benefit by Marital Status under Alternative Benchmark Scenarios, for the 1950 and 1985 Birth Cohorts

Benchmark	Cohort	Never married	Divorced	Married	Widowed
	Percentage change in median benefits for women whose benefits changed, benefits adjusted for household size				
Promised benefits	1950	0	-8.00	-2.67	15.58
	1985	0	-24.11	-9.01	18.91
Funded benefits	1950	0	-8.00	-2.67	15.58
	1985	0	-21.31	-8.98	20.75
	Percentage of women in each marital status whose benefits changed, benefits adjusted for householdsize				
Promised benefits	1950	0	12.84	35.89	13.92
	1985	0	11.91	34.19	11.11
Funded benefits	1950	0	12.80	35.57	13.92
	1985	0	13.13	33.96	20.22
	Percentage of total simulation population whose benefits changed, benefits adjusted for household size				
Promised benefits	1950	0	1.60	8.42	1.76
	1985	0	1.22	9.19	0.90
	Percentage change in median benefits for women whose benefits changed, benefits adjusted for household size				
Funded benefits	1950	0	1.60	8.35	1.76
	1985	0	1.34	9.13	1.64

Source: GAO analysis of GEMINI model.

Note: Simulations calculated benefits for individuals at age 70.

Table 26. Simulation Results for Reduced Marriage Requirement for Divorced Spouse Benefits under Alternative Benchmark Scenarios, for the 1950 and 1985 Birth Cohorts

	Reduced marriage requirement for divorced spouse benefits		
Benchmark	Cohort	All men	All women
	Median percentage change in median benefits for individuals whose benefits changed, benefits adjusted for household size		
Promised benefits	1950	0.85	65.32
	1985	37.22	45.05
Funded benefits	1950	0	65.32
	1985	40.51	47.97

	Percentage of specified subpopulation of simulated sample whose benefits changed, benefits adjusted for household size		
Promised benefits	1950	0	0.07
	1985	0.06	1.00
Funded benefits	1950	0	0.07
	1985	0.06	1.01
	Percentage of total simulation population whose benefits changed, benefits adjusted for household size		
Promised benefits	1950	0	0.04
	1985	0.03	0.51
Funded benefits	1950	0	0.04
	1985	0.03	0.52
	Percentage of specified subpopulation of simulated sample whose benefits changed, individual benefits not adjusted for household size		
Promised benefits	1950	0	0.06
	1985	0.06	0.96
Funded benefits	1950	0	0.06
	1985	0.06	0.97
	Percentage of total simulation population whose benefits changed, individual benefits not adjusted for household size		
Promised benefits	1950	0	0.03
	1985	0.03	0.49
Funded benefits	1950	0	0.03
	1985	0.03	0.50

Source: GAO analysis of GEMINI model.
Note: Simulations calculated benefits for individuals at age 70.

Table 27. Simulation Results for Reduced Marriage Requirement for Divorced Spouse Benefits by Income Quintile under Alternative Benchmark Scenarios, for the 1950 and 1985 Birth Cohorts

	Women only					
Benchmark	Cohort	Lowest quintile	Quintile 2	Middle quintile	Quintile 4	Highest quintile
	Percentage change in median benefits for individuals whose benefits changed, benefits adjusted for household size					
Promised benefits	1950	85.18	54.66	162.36	33.33	0
	1985	53.99	34.41	33.33	36.31	25.14
Funded benefits	1950	85.18	54.66	162.36	33.33	0
	1985	58.00	37.43	39.34	35.08	25.14
	Percentage of women in each income quintile whose benefits changed, benefits adjusted for household size					
Promised benefits	1950	0.07	0.13	0.06	0.05	0
	1985	2.46	1.13	0.70	0.33	0.08
Funded benefits	1950	0.07	0.13	0.06	0.05	0
	1985	2.44	1.17	0.70	0.35	0.08
	Percentage of total simulation population whose benefits changed, benefits adjusted for household size					
Promised benefits	1950	0.01	0.02	0.01	0	0
	1985	0.27	0.13	0.07	0.03	0.01
Funded benefits	1950	0.01	0.02	0.01	0	0
	1985	0.27	0.13	0.07	0.03	0.01

Source: GAO analysis of GEMINI model.
Note: Simulations calculated benefits for individuals at age 70. Income quintiles are based on the distribution of the present value of family lifetime earnings for the whole population (male and female).

Table 28. Simulation Results for Reduced Marriage Requirement for Divorced Spouse Benefits by Marital Status under Alternative Benchmark Scenarios, for the 1950 and 1985 Birth Cohorts

Women only					
Benchmark	Cohort	Never married	Divorced	Married	Widowed
	Percentage change in median benefitsfor women whose benefitschanged, benefitsadjusted for household size				
Promised benefits	1950	0	65.32	0	
	1985	0	45.05	0	0
Funded benefits	1950	0	65.32	0	
	1985	0	47.97	0	0
	Percentage of women in each marital statuswhose benefitschanged, benefitsadjusted for household size				
Promised benefits	1950	0	0.29	0	0
	1985	0	4.99		0
Funded benefits	1950	0	0.29	0	0
	1985	0	5.04	0	0
	Percentage of total simulation population whose benefitschanged, benefitsadjusted for household size				
Promised benefits	1950	0	0.04	0	0
	1985	0	0.51	0	0
Funded benefits	1950	0	0.04	0	0
	1985	0	0.52	0	0

Source: GAO analysis of GEMINI model.

Note: Simulations calculated benefits for individuals at age 70.

Table 29. Simulation Results for Increased Minimum Benefit under Alternative Benchmark Scenarios, for the 1950 and 1985 Birth Cohorts

Increased minimum benefit			
Benchmark	Cohort	All Men	All Women
	Percentage change in median benefitsfor individualswhose benefitschanged, benefitsadjusted for household size		
Promised benefits	1950	8.47	9.89
	1985	6.20	6.70
Funded benefits	1950	8.58	9.94
	1985	8.31	8.62
	Percentage of specified subpopulation of simulated sample whose benefitschanged, benefitsadjusted for household size		
Promised benefits	1950	16.68	16.30
	1985	2.43	2.48
Funded benefits	1950	17.02	16.45
	1985	13.66	12.57
	Percentage of total simulation population whose benefitschanged, benefitsadjusted for household size		
Promised benefits	1950	7.71	8.77
	1985	1.18	1.28
Funded benefits	1950	7.87	8.85

	1985	6.61	6.49
	Percentage of specified subpopulation of simulated sample whose benefitschanged, individual benefitsnot adjusted for household size		
Promised benefits	1950	10.60	14.47
	1985	1.79	1.79
Funded benefits	1950	10.63	14.54
	1985	10.28	9.03
	Percentage of total simulation population whose benefitschanged, individual benefitsnot adjusted for household size		
Promised benefits	1950	4.90	7.78
	1985	0.86	0.92
Funded benefits	1950	4.91	7.82
	1985	4.97	4.67

Source: GAO analysis of GEMINI model.

Note: Simulations calculated benefits for individuals at age 70.

Table 30. Simulation Results for Increased Minimum Benefit by Income Quintiles under Alternative Benchmark Scenarios, for the 1950 and 1985 Birth Cohorts

	Women only					
Benchmark	Cohort	Lowest quintile	Quintile 2	Middle quintile	Quintile 4	Highest quintile
	Percentage change in median benefits for individuals whose benefits changed, benefits adjusted for household size					
Promised benefits	1950	22.83	9.65	5.21	3.51	2.55
	1985	8.26	2.46	2.27	0.09	0
Funded benefits	1950	22.83	9.70	5.29	3.57	2.55
	1985	14.59	5.33	2.98	1.70	3.70*
	Percentage of women in each income quintile whose benefits changed, benefits adjusted for household size					
Promised benefits	1950	20.68	28.14	15.74	7.18	2.62
	1985	8.17	1.56	0.46	0.15	0.15
Funded benefits	1950	20.80	28.36	15.92	7.36	2.62
	1985	28.46	18.65	6.37	1.67	0.46
	Percentage of total simulation population whose benefits changed, benefits adjusted for household size					
Promised benefits	1950	2.85	3.38	1.65	0.69	0.21
	1985	1.03	0.17	0.05	0.01	0.01
Funded benefits	1950	2.87	3.40	1.66	0.71	0.21
	1985	3.60	2.03	0.66	0.16	0.04

Source: GAO analysis of GEMINI model.

Note: Simulations calculated benefits for individuals at age 70. Income quintiles are based on the distribution of the present value of family lifetime earnings for the whole population (male and female). *Contrary to the pattern for the 1950 cohort, the median change for the highest income quintile of the 1985 cohort among women who had a simulated benefit change is larger than the median change for some of the other income quintiles. The median change in this quintile, however, is consistent with our assessment from both cohorts that higher median changes occur in lower income quintiles. Also, it is worth noting that in the highest income quintile, women who had simulated benefit changes accounted for less than 0.25 percent of the population in each cohort.

Table 31. Simulation Results for Increased Minimum Benefit by Marital Status under Alternative Benchmark Scenarios, for the 1950 and 1985 Birth Cohorts

Women only					
Benchmark	Cohort	Never married	Divorced	Married	Widowed
	Percentage change in median benefitsfor women whose benefitschanged, benefitsadjusted for household size				
Promised benefits	1950	22.80	17.13	7.43	8.34
	1985	19.01	14.50	4.55	6.48
Funded benefits	1950	22.80	17.14	7.46	8.40
	1985	20.53	15.21	6.87	8.34
	Percentage of women in each marital statuswhose benefitschanged, benefitsadjusted for household size				
Promised benefits	1950	16.97	14.87	17.52	15.17
	1985	2.93	2.00	2.82	1.59
Funded benefits	1950	16.97	14.88	17.83	15.21
	1985	9.84	9.45	15.01	10.48
	Percentage of total simulation population whose benefitschanged, benefitsadjusted for household size				
Promised benefits	1950	0.81	1.91	4.19	1.86
	1985	0.18	0.21	0.76	0.13
Funded benefits	1950	0.81	1.91	4.27	1.87
	1985	0.61	0.99	4.06	0.84

Source: GAO analysis of GEMINI model.
Note: Simulations calculated benefits for individuals at age 70.

APPENDIX III: LOW BENEFIT AVOIDANCE RATES

The low benefit avoidance rate is expressed as the percent of retirement years in which an individual's Social Security benefits (plus any earnings) are above a low-benefit threshold (set at $9,669 for individuals and $12,186 for couples, in 2007 dollars). Both income and the threshold are based on individual data when unmarried and on couple data when married.

Table 32. Average Low Benefit Avoidance Rates Before and After Modifications for Individuals with Less Than 100 Percent Low Benefit Avoidance Pre-Modification

	Promised benefits(tax increase only) benchmark									
	1950 cohort					1985 cohort				
Social Security modification	All women	Never married	Divorced	Married	Widowed	All women	Never married	Divorced	Married	Widowed
Current law (no reform)	17.05	0.06	9.77	37.41	11.77	19.21	0	8.87	42.18	12.53
Dependent care credit	21.18	1.33	13.50	42.27	17.70	24.49	1.50	13.32	49.46	20.15
Increased survivor benefit only	23.11	0.06	12.22	47.35	23.16	25.59	0	11.47	53.40	24.79
Decreased spousal benefit with increased survivor benefit	22.76	0.06	11.91	46.75	22.89	24.10	0	9.95	50.83	24.01
Decreased marriage requirement	17.14	0.06	10.03	37.41	11.77	20.72	0	13.57	42.18	12.53
Increased minimum benefit	23.18	6.88	15.29	42.80	19.73	19.66	0	8.87	43.36	12.80
Current law (no reform)	17.00	0.06	9.63	37.32	11.79	14.82	0	5.83	30.51	7.84
Dependent care credit	21.17	1.33	13.38	42.28	17.70	17.72	0.42	7.52	35.44	10.59
Increased survivor benefit only	23.09	0.06	12.12	47.30	23.17	21.02	0	8.82	40.26	18.01
Decreased spousal benefit with increased survivor benefit	22.67	0.06	11.68	46.60	22.90	20.12	0	8.55	38.37	17.48
Decreased marriage requirement	17.10	0.06	9.89	37.32	11.79	15.51	0	8.23	30.51	7.84
Increased minimum benefit	23.20	6.88	15.18	42.88	19.78	16.58	0	5.84	34.85	8.23

Source: GAO analysis based on GEMINI model.

Note: Simulations calculated benefits for individuals at age 70.

APPENDIX IV: EFFECT OF SIMULATED REFORM ON SOCIAL SECURITY SYSTEM SOLVENCY

Table 33. Changes in the 75-year Actuarial Balance as a Percentage of Taxable Payroll resulting from Program Modifications, after Achieving 75-Year Solvency with Benchmark Scenarios

Modification	Promised benefits(tax increase only)	Funded benefits(proportional benefitreduction only)
Dependent care credit	-0.17	-0.19
Increased survivor benefit only	-0.07	-0.14
Increased survivor benefit with decreased spousal benefit	0.02	-0.06
Reduced marriage requirement (from 10 years to 7 years)	-0.02	-0.06
Increased minimum benefit	-0.05	-0.13

Source: GAO analysis of SSASIM model..

REFERENCES

[1] The Board of Trustees, Federal Old-Age and Survivors Insurance and Disability Insurance Trust Funds, The 2007 Annual Report of the Board of Trustees of the Federal Old-Age and Survivors Insurance and Disability Insurance Trust Funds (Washington, D.C.: Apr. 23, 2007).

[2] Family structure changed substantially during the later part of the 20th century. According to the Census Bureau, in 1970, about 70 percent of all households were composed of married couple families. By 2003, this had fallen to less than 52 percent. In addition, the proportion of families with children that were headed by a single parent increased from 13 percent in 1970 to 32 percent in 2003.

[3] We used the GEMINI model under a license from the Policy Simulation Group, a private contractor. GEMINI estimates individual effects of policy scenarios for a representative sample of future beneficiaries. GEMINI can simulate different reform features for their effects on the level and distribution of benefits. See appendix I for more detail on the modeling analysis, including a discussion of our assessment of the data reliability of the model.

[4] We did not simulate pension benefits for the 1950 birth cohort because the current version of PENSIM does not have a realistic characterization of pre-1996 employer pension offerings, and therefore should not be used to simulate lifetime pension accumulation for cohorts born before 1975.

[5] There are both advantages and disadvantages of using such measures. For additional information on the development, use, and limitations of equivalence scales see, Constance F. Citro and Robert T. Michael (eds.), Measuring Poverty: A New Approach, Washington, DC: National Academy Press, 1995 and GAO, Social Security: Program's Role in Helping Ensure Income Adequacy, GAO-02-62 (Washington, D.C.: Nov 30, 2001).

[6] For more information on our adjustment of income, see appendix I.

[7] This variable is called the "low benefit avoidance rate." It is produced by the model and is expressed as a percentage of retirement years in which Social Security benefits (plus any earnings) are above a predetermined low benefit threshold. The threshold is measured separately for married couples and for unmarried individuals. It does not include pension income or savings, and so cannot be called a true poverty-avoidance measure.

[8] See appendix I for a complete description of our benchmark policy scenarios.

[9] The Board of Trustees, Federal Old-Age and Survivors Insurance and Disability Insurance Trust Funds, The 2007 Annual Report of the Board of Trustees of the Federal Old-Age and Survivors Insurance and Disability Insurance Trust Funds.

[10] Also, some proposals would change the structure of the program to incorporate a system of individual accounts. Many such proposals would reduce benefits under the current system and make up for those reductions to some degree with income from the individual accounts.

[11] Although DC plans generally are not required to have an annuity option, certain DC plans, known as money purchase plans, are required to make an annuity payout option available to participants. In addition, lump sum distributions from DB plans are becoming more common.

[12] The difference in annuity benefits for men and women exists only for private annuities. In 1983, the U.S. Supreme Court held that an employer's use of sex-segregated actuarial tables to calculate retirement benefits is unlawful, whether or not the tables reflect an accurate prediction of the longevity of women as a class. Arizona Governing Comm. for Tax Deferred Annuity and Deferred Compensation Plans v. Norris, 463 U.S. 1073, 1084 (1983).

[13] GAO analysis of National Income and Product Accounts (NIPA) data from the Bureau of Economic Analysis (BEA). Personal saving, as measured in the NIPA, does not include capital gains on existing assets because capital gains reflect a revaluation of the nation's existing capital stock and do not provide resources for financing investment that adds to the capital stock. In other words, although an individual household can tap its wealth by selling assets to finance consumption or accumulate other assets, the sale of an existing asset merely transfers ownership; it does not generate new economic output.

[14] In 2006 and 2007, an individual may make a contribution of up to $4,000 annually to a spousal IRA. The contribution amount increases to $5,000 in 2008 and will be adjusted based on inflation after that. In addition, those over age 50 are permitted to contribute an additional $1,000 per year.

[15] The Kaiser/HRET Employer Health Benefits 2001 to 2006 Annual Surveys found that between 2001 and 2006 the share of employers with 200 or more workers offering retiree health benefits remained relatively steady, with about 35 percent offering retiree health benefits in 2006. Survey data also show that retiree health benefits are most likely offered by large or unionized firms.

[16] People aged 85 or more are much more likely to be covered only by Medicare than those in the 65-74 age category.

[17] However, women make up the majority of the poor elderly recipients of the Supplemental Security Income program—a joint federal-state poverty program

designed to help the elderly (and the blind and disabled of all ages), who have little or no income, meet their basic needs for food, clothing, and shelter.

[18] Patrick Purcell, Topics in Aging: Income of Americans Age 65 and Older, 1969 to 2004 (Washington, D.C.: Congressional Research Service, 2006).

[19] The Census Bureau's Current Population Survey, measures the sources and amount of income people receive. It does not, however, measure a person's wealth, which would include the total amount of lifetime savings. Consequently, in this report, asset income refers to income received from interest or dividends earned on savings, as well as rents and royalties from other types of property.

[20] If the worker is covered by a DB plan or by certain DC plans, such as a money purchase plan, the pension plan is required to obtain the written consent of the worker's spouse if the worker declines the qualified joint and survivor annuity option.

[21] A joint and survivor annuity provides income to the surviving spouse should the retired worker die first. However, one study found that 28 percent of married men and 69 percent of married women opted for single life annuities instead of joint and survivor annuities. See Richard W. Johnson, Cori E. Uccello, and Joshua H. Goldwyn, Single Life vs. Joint and Survivor Pension Payout Options: How Do Married Retirees Choose? The Urban Institute, September 2003.

[22] People and families are classified as poor if their income is less than the federal poverty level. The official weighted average poverty threshold in 2005 for a single person age 65 or older was $9,367. For a two-person household in which at least one member was at least 65 years old, the poverty threshold was $11,815.

[23] While the decline in men's labor force participation occurred in most age groups, it was more rapid among those aged 55 years and older.

[24] Mitra Toossi, "A New Look at Long-Term Labor Force Projections to 2050," *Monthly Labor Review*, vol. 129, no.11 (November 2006).

[25] GAO, Women's Earnings: Work Patterns Partially Explain Difference between Men's and Women's Earnings, GAO-04-35 (Washington, D.C.: Oct. 31, 2003).

[26] U.S. Department of Labor, Bureau of Labor Statistics, Women in the Labor Force: A Databook, Report 996 (Washington, D.C.: September 2006).

[27] U.S. Department of Labor, Bureau of Labor Statistics, Women in the Labor Force: A Databook.

[28] GAO-04-35.

[29] Alicia Munnell and Pamela Perun, "An Update on Private Pensions," Issue Brief No. 50 (Center for Retirement Research, Boston College: August 2006).

[30] Employee Benefit Research Institute, "Employment-Based Retirement Plan Participation: Geographic Differences and Trends, 2005," Issue Brief No. 299, November 2006.

[31] More than 19 million women aged 65 and older received benefits for December 2005. About 39 percent were entitled solely to a retired worker benefit. Almost 30 percent were dually entitled to a retired worker benefit and a wife's or widow's benefit. About 31 percent were receiving wife's or widow's benefits only.

[32] Benefit levels are determined by averaging the highest 35 years of indexed covered earnings. Years spent out of the labor force are represented by zeros. Consequently, an intermittent work history and lower wages result in a lower benefit level.

[33] Janet Wilmoth and Gregor Koso, "Does Marital History Matter? Marital Status and Wealth Outcomes among Pre-Retirement Adults," *Journal of Marriage and Family* 64 (February 2002): 254-268; Patricia A. McManus and Thomas A. DiPrete, "Losers and Winners: The Financial Consequences of Separation and Divorce for Men," *American Sociological Review* 66, no. 2 (April 2001): 246-268; Richard W. Johnson, Gordon B.T. Mermin, and Cori E. Uccello, When the Nest Egg Cracks: Financial Consequences of Health Problems, Marital Status Changes, and Job Layoffs at Older Ages, (Urban Institute: January 2006).

[34] Rose M. Kreider, "Number, Timing, and Duration of Marriages and Divorces: 2001," *Current Population Reports* P70-97, (U.S. Census Bureau, Washington, D.C.: February 2005); Richard Peterson, "A Re-Evaluation of the Economic Consequences of Divorce," *American Sociological Review* 61, no. 3 (June 1996): 528-536; Jay D. Teachman and Kathleen M. Paasch, "Financial Impact of Divorce on Children and Their Families," *The Future of Children* 4, no. 1, (Spring 1994): 63-83; Karen C. Holden and Pamela J. Smock, "The Economic Costs of Marital Dissolution: Why Do Women Bear a Disproportionate Cost?" *Annual Review of Sociology* 17 (1991): 51-78.

[35] Kreider. *Number, Timing, and Duration of Marriages and Divorces:* 2001, 13.

[36] Jacqueline L. Angel, Cynthia J. Buckley, Ronald J. Angel and Maren A. Jimenez, The Economic Consequences of Marital Disruption for Pre-Retirement Age: African-American, Hispanic and Non-Hispanic White Women, University of Texas at Austin. Paper presented at the Population Association of America Annual Meeting, Minneapolis, Minnesota (May 2003).

[37] Barbara A. Butrica and Howard M. Iams, "Divorced Women at Retirement: Projections of Economic Well-Being in the Near Future," *Social Security Bulletin* 63, no. 3 (2000): 8.

[38] While the majority of women receive Social Security retirement benefits based, at least in part, on their own work record, among women age 65 and older who received Social Security benefits in December 2005, 31 percent received benefits based exclusively on their marital history, and about 30 percent were "dually entitled"; i.e., benefits were based on both their own work record and their marital history. In comparison, the percentage of women who received divorced spousal benefits was relatively small. Whereas close to 15 million women received benefits as a retired worker in December 2005, less than 500,000 received benefits as either a divorced spouse or divorced widow. See Social Security Administration, Annual Statistical Supplement to the Social Security Bulletin, 2006, SSA Publication No. 13-11700, Washington, D.C., June 2007, pp. 2, 5.3, 5.10, and 5.17.

[39] Kreider. *Number, Timing, and Duration of Marriages and Divorces*: 2001," 9.

[40] The Employee Retirement Income Security Act of 1974, as amended, governs areas such as pension coverage, vesting periods, benefit accrual and distribution, and survivor's benefits.

[41] Pub. L. No. 98-397.

[42] 29 U.S.C. § 1056(d)(3).

[43] Unpaid leave includes all unpaid maternity, sick, and vacation leave, and other unpaid leave. See Julia Overturf Johnson and Barbara Downs, "Maternity Leave and Employment Patterns of First-Time Mothers: 1961-2000," *Current Population Reports* P70-103, U.S. Census Bureau, Washington, D.C., October 2005, p. 9.

[44] U.S. Department of Labor, Bureau of Labor Statistics, Women in the Labor Force: A Databook, Report 996 (Washington, D.C.: September 2006).

[45] Richard W. Johnson and Joshua M. Wiener, "A Profile of Frail Older Americans and Their Caregivers," Occasional Paper 8, Urban Institute: (February 2006).

[46] Institute for Women's Policy Research, "The Widening Gap: A New Book on the Struggle to Balance Work and Caregiving," Research in Brief C349 (October 2001).

[47] Courtney C. Coile, "Health Shocks and Couples' Labor Supply Decisions," National Bureau of Economic Research Working Paper 10810 (September 2004).

[48] Mature Market Institute at Metropolitan Life Insurance Company, MetLife Juggling Act Study: Balancing Caregiving with Work and the Costs Involved. Findings from a National Study by the National Alliance for Caregiving and the National Center on Women and Aging at Brandeis University (November 1999); National Alliance for Caregiving and AARP, Caregiving in the U.S. (April 2004); Genworth Financial, The Impact of Long Term Care on Women–An Analysis of Women as Care Providers and Care Recipients, 2006.

[49] Chizuko Wakabayashi and Katharine M. Donato, "The Consequences of Caregiving: Effects on Women's Employment and Earnings," *Population Research and Policy Review* 24, no. 5, (October 2005): 482.

[50] Other factors, such as education, marital status, and race, appear to be correlated with whether the female caregivers live in poverty. See Chizuko Wakabayashi and Katherine M. Donato, "Does Caregiving Increase Poverty in Later Life? Evidence from the Health and Retirement Survey." *Journal of Health and Social Behavior* 47 (September 2006): 264.

[51] Richard W. Johnson, Gordon B.T. Mermin, and Cori E. Uccello, "How secure are retirement nest eggs?" Issue in Brief No. 45, Center for Retirement Research at Boston College (April 2006); Purvi Sevak, David R. Weir, and Robert J. Willis, "The Economic Consequences of a Husband's Death: Evidence from the HRS and AHEAD," Social Security Bulletin 65, no. 3 (2003/2004): 31-44; and Catherine D. Zick and Karen Holden, "An Assessment of the Wealth Holdings of Recent Widows," *Journal of Gerontology: Social Sciences* 55B, no. 2 (2000): S90-S97. Note: While research has shown that widowhood increases the incidence of poverty among women who were not poor when married, some research indicates that many widows in poverty also had poor economic status in marriage as well. (See, Sevak, Weir, and Willis, "The Economic Consequences of a Husband's Death"; Zick and Holden, "An Assessment of the Wealth Holdings of Recent Widows.")

[52] A widow or widower who meets eligibility requirements is entitled to receive a percentage of the deceased spouse's Social Security benefits ("survivor benefits") or benefits based on his or her own work history—whichever is greater. Generally, the survivor is entitled to a benefit in the amount of the deceased spouse's PIA. However, the survivor's benefit amount may be reduced if the deceased spouse retired before reaching full retirement age, or increased if the deceased spouse delayed retirement beyond the full retirement age.

[53] Federal Interagency Forum on Aging-Related Statistics. Older Americans Update 2006: Key Indicators of Well-Being. Federal Interagency Forum on Aging-Related Statistics. Washington, D.C.: U.S. Government Printing Office, May 2006, p. 29.

[54] Jeffrey R. Brown and Amy Finkelstein, "Supply or Demand: Why is the Market for Long- Term Care Insurance So Small?" National Bureau of Economic Research, Working Paper 10782 (September 2004).

[55] Adrienne Jones, The National Nursing Home Survey: 1999 summary. National Center for Health Statistics. Vital Health Stat 13(152). 2002; Current Home Health Care Patients. National Center for Health Care Statistics, Centers for Disease Control and Prevention, February 2004. http://www.cdc.gov/nchs/about/major/ nhhcsd/nhhc shomecare3.htm

[56] Kathleen McGarry and Robert F. Schoeni, "Medicare Gaps and Widow Poverty," Social Security Bulletin 66, no. 1, (2005) and Genworth Financial, The Impact of Long Term Care on Women; Johnson, Mermin, and Uccello, "When the Nest Egg Cracks."

[57] Genworth Financial, The Impact of Long Term Care on Women.

[58] McGarry and Schoeni, "Medicare Gaps and Widow Poverty."

[59] Under the "Promised Benefits" benchmark, the "increased survivor benefits with decreased spousal benefits" modification resulted in a positive impact on the 75 year actuarial balance. For all solvency results, see appendix IV.

[60] For more information on the Policy Simulation Group's models, see appendix I.

[61] Outcomes from each reform could be different for individuals at ages other than 70, particularly as the incidence of widowhood in the population increases at higher ages.

[62] Melissa Faverault and Eugene Steuerle, Social Security Spouse and Survivor Benefits for the Modern Family (Washington DC: Urban Institute, 2006).

[63] Melissa Favreault and Frank Sammartino, The Impact of Social Security Reform on Low-Income and Older Women (Washington D.C.: Urban Institute, 2002).

[64] Some dependent care proposals might also provide enhanced benefits to individuals caring for dependent adults. However, for ease of modeling we simulated a proposal in which the benefits were limited to those with young dependent children. Proposals that do include benefits for adult caregivers would likely affect a larger number of beneficiaries than the version we simulated.

[65] Individuals in the sample population that met these criteria were credited with one-half of average wages (as measured by the Average Wage Index used by the Social Security Administration) for up to 5 years. If both parents meet these criteria in any given year, only the lower-earning parent would receive the credit; if parents had identical earnings, the credit is split evenly. The credit would not contribute to quarters of coverage for eligibility purposes. The design of this reform effectively would provide a limited minimum benefit for workers with children under 5.

[66] We used the 1950 and 1985 simulated birth cohorts in all of the simulations of Social Security reform elements presented in this report.

[67] This reform would reduce the 75-year solvency achieved by the "promised benefits" benchmark by 0.19 percent. The "promised benefits" benchmark achieves 75-year solvency by increasing payroll taxes by the amount of Social Security's actuarial deficit as a percentage of payroll. For more information on this and the "funded benefits" benchmark see appendix I. For a summary of the solvency impact of all simulated modification under both the "promised benefits" and the "funded benefits" benchmarks see appendix IV.

[68] Previous to the Special Primary Insurance Amount, Social Security had a Minimum Benefit that did not target lifetime low earners; this benefit was criticized for providing

windfall benefits for workers with only a minimal attachment to the Social Security system.

[69] See Office of the Chief Actuary, Social Security Administration, Estimated OASDI Financial Effects of the "Bipartisan Retirement Security Act of 2005" (Nov. 4, 2005) at http://www.ssa.gov/OACT/solvency/Kolbe_20051104.pdf.

[70] For data, see appendix II, table 30.

[71] The increased minimum benefit, as we've modeled it, would reduce the 75-year actuarial balance achieved by the "Promised benefits" benchmark by 0.05 percent. For more information on this and the "Funded benefits" benchmark, see appendix I. For a summary of the solvency impact of all simulated reforms under both the "Promised benefits" and the "Funded benefits" benchmarks see appendix IV.

[72] A potential unintended consequence of a more generous minimum benefit is that higher benefits may disqualify certain individuals from Supplemental Security Income (SSI) eligibility. This is significant for some beneficiaries living in states that provide automatic Medicaid eligibility for SSI recipients.

[73] For the 1985 cohort, this reform had an impact on twice the number of widows in the "Funded benefits" framework than in the "Promised benefits" framework; this is because the "Funded benefits" results in lower benefit levels and more survivors have incomes below the cap of average PIA.

[74] As simulated, this change would reduce the 75-year solvency achieved by the "Promised benefits" benchmark by 0.07 percent. For more information on this and the "Funded benefits" benchmark see appendix I. For a summary of the solvency impact of all simulated changes under both the "Promised benefits" and the "Funded benefits" benchmarks see appendix IV.

[75] Based on our simulation, this change would improve the 75-year actuarial balance achieved by the "Promised benefits" benchmark by 0.02 percent. The "Funded benefits" benchmark does not fully offset; the solvency impact of this reform on the "Funded benefits" benchmark is -0.06%

[76] In 1995, 30 percent of marriages ended in divorce within the first 10 years.

[77] Based on our simulation, this change would reduce the 75-year solvency achieved by the "Promised benefits" benchmark by 0.02 percent of payroll.

[78] Pension reforms were modeled using only the 1985 cohort, as PENSIM model data are not valid for cohorts born before 1975 (per PENSIM documentation).

[79] Defined benefit plans promise to provide a benefit that is generally based on an employee's salary and years of service. Defined contribution plans have individual accounts to which the employer, employees, or both make periodic contributions. For more information, see GAO, Answers to Key Questions about Private Pension Plans, GAO-02-745SP (Washington, D.C.: Sept.18, 2002).

[80] Plans with cliff vesting have a specified point at which participants have a right to benefits accrued to date and benefits accrued thereafter. For more information, see GAO-02-745SP.

[81] Plans with graduated vesting give participants a right to an increasing percentage of their total accrued benefit over time. For more information, see GAO-02-745SP.

[82] The Pension Protection Act of 2006 accelerated some vesting requirements for DC plans.

[83] One survey found that the most frequently cited reason for not participating in a retirement plan when a plan was offered by employers was an insufficient period of employment (39 percent of male employees versus 35 percent of female employees).

[84] We simulated pension income only for the 1985 birth cohort because the current version of PENSIM does not have a realistic characterization of pre-1996 employer pension offerings and therefore should not be used to simulate lifetime pension accumulation for cohorts born before 1975.

[85] "Lump-Sum Distributions," EBRI Notes, Volume 16, no.12 (Employee Benefit Research Institute, December 2005).

[86] While these models use sample data, our report, like others using these models, does not address the issue of sampling errors. The results of the analysis reflect outcomes for individuals in the simulated populations and do not attempt to estimate outcomes for an actual population.

[87] MINT3 is a detailed microsimulation model developed jointly by the Social Security Administration, the Brookings Institution, RAND, and the Urban Institute to project the distribution of income in retirement for the 1931 to 1960 birth cohorts.

[88] We did not simulate pension benefits for the 1950 birth cohort because the current version of PENSIM does not have a realistic characterization of pre-1996 employer pension offerings, and therefore, should not be used to simulate lifetime pension accumulation for cohorts born before 1975.

[89] See GAO, Social Security: Criteria for Evaluating Reform Proposals, GAO/T-HEHS-99-94 (Washington, D.C.: Mar. 25, 1999), and GAO, Social Security: Evaluating Reform Proposals, GAO/AIMD/HEHS-00-29 (Washington, D.C.: Nov. 4, 1999).

[90] For a discussion of individual equity issues, see GAO, Social Security: Issues in Comparing Rates of Return with Market Investments, GAO/HEHS-99-110 (Washington, D.C.: Aug. 5, 1999).

[91] GAO-02-62.

[92] The Board of Trustees, Federal Old-Age and Survivors Insurance and Disability Insurance Trust Funds, The 2007 Annual Report of the Board of Trustees of the Federal Old-Age and Survivors Insurance and Federal Disability Insurance Trust Funds (Washington, D.C.: Apr. 23, 2007).

[93] There are both advantages and disadvantages of using such measures. For additional information on the development, use, and limitations of equivalence scales see, Constance F. Citro and Robert T. Michael (eds.), Measuring Poverty: A New Approach, Washington, DC: National Academy Press, 1995, and GAO, Social Security: Program's Role in Helping Ensure Income Adequacy, GAO-02-62 (Washington, D.C.: Nov 30, 2001).

[94] This change is similar to one scored by OCACT as part of the 1994-96 Advisory Council Report, which estimates a 0.32 percent increase to the long-range actuarial deficit. However, the OCACT scoring of the similar change in the 1994-96 Advisory Council Report did not include a cap at the level of average benefits, so the impact on long-range solvency was greater. A capped version of an increase in survivors' benefits was presented as part of Estimates of Financial Effects for Three Models Developed by the President's Commission to Strengthen Social Security in January 2002; for these outcomes, please see the description of "increase survivor benefit" change.

[95] These benchmarks were first developed for our report GAO-02-62. We have since used them in other studies, including GAO-03-310; GAO, Social Security Reform: Analysis of a Trust Fund Exhaustion Scenario, GAO-03-907 (Washington, D.C.: July 29, 2003); GAO, Social Security and Minorities: Earnings, Disability Incidence, and Mortality Are Key Factors That Influence Taxes Paid and Benefits Received, GAO-03-387 (Washington, D.C.: Apr. 23, 2003); GAO-04-747; and GAO, Social Security Reform: Implications of Different Indexing Choices, GAO-06-804 (Washington, D.C.: Sept. 14, 2006).

[96] The Social Security actuaries provided these scorings for a previous report and used assumptions from the 2001 trustees' report. The actuaries did not believe it was necessary to provide new scorings using updated assumptions for the purposes of our study, since the assumptions and the estimates of actuarial balance on which they are based have changed little from the 2001 report. In particular, they did not believe that the differences in assumptions would materially affect the shape of the distribution of benefits, which is the focus of our analysis. All estimates related to the indexing scenarios and benchmark policy scenarios were simulated using the SSASIM OLC mode.

[97] Advisory Council on Social Security. Report of the 1994-1996 Advisory Council on Social Security, Vols. 1 and 2. Washington, D.C.: Jan. 1997.

[98] See GAO-03-907, in which we analyzed such a policy scenario under a congressional request.

[99] The highest 35 years of salary are used in the calculation of a retired worker benefit. The disabled worker benefit is calculated using the number of years between the age of entitlement and age 21, divided by 5.

[100] Other analyses have addressed the concern about the effect of the proportional reduction on low earners by modifying that offset to apply only to the 32 and 15 percent formula factors. The MTR policy in the 1994 to 1996 Advisory Council report used this approach, which in turn was based on the individual account (IA) proposal in that report. However, the MTR policy also reflected other changes in addition to PIA formula changes.

INDEX

A

B

H

I

J

K

L

M

N

O

P

Q

R

S

T

U

V

W